CW00691388

CRICKET'S BIGGEST MYSTERY:

THE ASHES

CRICKET'S BIGGEST MYSTERY:

THE ASHES

Ronald Willis

LUTTERWORTH PRESS
GUILDFORD, SURREY

For Ruth Natasha
who doesn't
understand yet

ISBN 0-7188-2588-8

LUTTERWORTH PRESS edition 1983

Rigby Publishers • Adelaide • Australia
First published by Rigby Publishers 1982
Copyright © 1982 Ronald Willis

All rights reserved
Wholly designed and typeset in Australia
Printed by Bright Sun Printing Press Co Ltd in Hong Kong

'. . . the Ashes, the trophy, a wooden urn containing a cremated cricket stump, kept permanently in England, played for by England and Australia in Test cricket . . .'

The Macquarie Dictionary, 1981

CHAPTER 1

In pursuit of the truth about the Ashes and the people who were involved in their creation, it is necessary to examine events and their circumstances half the world apart in England and Australia 100 years ago. This investigation indicates that contrary to the popular legend, Ivo Bligh was given the Ashes *before* he 'recovered' them by virtue of his Test-match exploits.

The saga was unintentionally started with a Test match in 1882 between England and Australia which, in prospect, seemed unlikely to be remembered 100 years later. It was played in England on one of the scattered properties of the Duchy of Cornwall — owned since the thirteenth century by the Prince of Wales — better known as Kennington Oval, London.

In 1882, English cricket enthusiasts had little, if any, doubt about the result of the encounter. England always beat the Australians on English soil. Scheduled for three days, it began on Monday, 28 August.

Legend in the making can be traced from the point on the second day when Doctor William Gilbert Grace was dismissed and England needed 32 runs to win with six wickets to fall. If ever the ending of a game deserved to be televised, this did — but there was no television then, nor radio. What would Alan McGilvray and John Arlott have made of it? The hush at times was louder than that in Sir Henry Newboult's Close.

Many retrospective observers of this historic encounter have attributed to the tension the death of one spectator from a heart attack and, to another watcher, the feat of biting through the handle of his umbrella. While the umbrella incident is not disputed, two newspapers of the day recorded the fatality and agreed that the man who died collapsed shortly after the close of the Australians' second innings — before the most exciting part developed.

Australia, of course, won, and the fast bowler, Frederick Robert 'Demon' Spofforth was chaired from the field with match figures of fourteen for 90. Soon afterwards, the *Sporting Times* lamented 'the death of English cricket.' This was the cynically-humorous inspiration of a young London journalist called Reginald Brooks perhaps as, with other Englishmen, shocked and in mourning, he drowned his sorrows in a tavern. The Ashes had been conceived . . .

The *Wisden Cricketers' Almanack*, 100 years later, still attributes the lament to 'Shirley Brooks, son of an editor of *Punch* (magazine),' while Marylebone Cricket Club, in its explanation of the Ashes, ignores him, referring merely to the *Sporting Times*.

In fact, Shirley Brooks, once described by a contemporary as having 'the brilliantest pen in London' had been dead for eight years when his eldest son, Reginald, coined the Ashes.

Reginald thus unwittingly ensured the revival of his own memory — and that of the Hon. Ivo Bligh who was still hovering in the wings — by the

The Ashes urn with the velvet bag

curious for as long as sparks are struck on a cricket field in battles for the Ashes between England and Australia.

Let us next rid ourselves, then, of the confusion over these names which has been perpetuated by various authorities down the decades.

The editor of *Punch* in question was properly called Charles William Shirley Brooks, but he always preferred to be called Shirley and dropped his first two names as soon as he was able.

The eldest son of Shirley and Emily Brooks was called Reginald Shirley Watkinshaw and was normally referred to as Reginald or, within his family circle, as Reg, or Rego; never Shirley, for the obvious reason.

Shirley Brooks, in his heyday, was a fashionable journalist, author and playwright. His plays were performed successfully in many of the West End theatres in London.

Ivo Bligh

The eldest of three sons of a London freeman, goldsmith and architect, he was born on 29 April 1816, at 52 Doughty Street — the same street in which Charles Dickens worked on *The Pickwick Papers* and *David Copperfield*.

Shirley was trained by his uncle, Charles Sabine, at Oswestry, to be a solicitor, but abandoned this promising career to become a journalist, his more natural bent.

On 1 June 1853, he recorded in his diary proposing to Emily Marguerite Watkinshaw. He was thirty-seven and she twenty-two.

A daughter of Dr William Bannatyre Watkinshaw, of Naparima, Trinidad, Emily was a brunette and, though technically a Creole, was Irish and proud of it. She had a blonde sister and the pair were known to the fashionable art and literary set as 'Night and Morning.' They were painted as such by Carl Schiller.

9

Shirley Brooks

Shirley and Emily were married in the summer of 1854. They made their home at 6 Kent Terrace (still occupied), off Baker Street, and, by chance, only a few minutes' walk from Lord's.

Their first child, Reginald, was born that autumn, 12 October 1854. Three years later, on 20 August 1857 — a few months after the birth of Oscar Wilde — Emily produced their second and last child, Cecil Cunningham.

Cecil's name was the first to be entered in the register at Summer Fields, the Oxford preparatory school that was opened in 1864 and still functions today.

The Brooks boys were followed there by the nephew and two sons of Alexander Macmillan, the founder of the publishing company. Boy No. 892 was the former British Conservative Prime Minister, Mr Harold Macmillan.

From Summer Fields, Reginald and Cecil went to the now defunct International College, Isleworth, in which their father apparently invested and lost some money.

Cecil, it seems, ended his schooldays at Isleworth, but Reginald, who, at one point, was expelled from there for 'rebellion' and reinstated, showed great potential.

In January 1871, Reginald went to Owens College, Manchester, and from there, two years later, to Heidélburg where his studies were halted by illness.

His mother, Emily, sped to his bedside and Shirley was prepared to go, but this became unnecessary as Reginald gradually recovered and returned with his mother to London.

Shirley's death on 23 February 1874, at the age of fifty-eight was from a combination of bronchitis and dropsy. It marked the beginning of the family's decline and slide towards tragic circumstances.

Mrs Brooks moved with her sons from the fine house in Kent Terrace to another in Bentinck Terrace, a coach-building district, also off Baker Street but in a less fashionable area and nearer the city. She died six years later on 14 May 1880, and was buried beside her husband in Kensal Green Cemetery. She was forty-nine.

Shirley's papers and diaries, safe enough while Emily lived, were gradually squandered, some of them apparently hawked around London by either Reginald or Cecil to be parted with for a few miserable shillings.

M. H. Spielmann, in his history of *Punch*, wrote: 'Reginald Shirley Brooks . . . was working for *Punch* in 1880, and the following year he was called to the Table, and there remained, without much distinction, until 1884. He wrote some smart papers, but his groove was not the sober and respectable Fleet Street sage. He preferred wilder spirits, and he accordingly retired, taking with him the sympathy of his companions. He died soon after.'

This brusque dismissal of Reginald was elaborated on, but only marginally, in 1907 by George Soames Layard: '. . . Then (after retiring from *Punch*) he blossomed into "Blobbs" of the *Sporting Times* and his fate was sealed.

'Those were the days when certain "smart" drinking bars in London stood free to that poisonous group of dissipated flaneurs who posed as the latest expression of sporting journalism and simulated every vice which they did not practise.

'"About this time," writes one of his acquaintances, "he fell madly in love with a well-known actress, who is now a peeress, and tried to shoot himself, but failing, was not too overcome to give a laughable account of it to his friends." This is, in little, the record of a wasted life. The end was certain, and, like many another of his colleagues, he went under and died.'

In Affectionate Remembrance

OF

ENGLISH CRICKET,

WHICH DIED AT THE OVAL

ON

29th AUGUST, 1882,

Deeply lamented by a large circle of sorrowing friends and acquaintances.

R. I. P.

N.B.—The body will be cremated and the ashes taken to Australia.

The mock obituary notice from the *Sporting Times*

Layard went on: 'The history of the younger boy was no less tragic, and the only satisfaction in the whole wretched business was that the passionately devoted father did not live long enough to see his fondest hopes dashed to the ground . . .'

Layard also examined some of Reginald's diaries. Of these, he said: '. . . All too soon, the canker of self-indulgence and irresponsibility shows up as we read between the lines.

'The petty triumphs of the billiard and card-table take the place of high ambition and worthy emulation, and he who should have been the master of

12

his fate, quickly exhibited himself the slave of his passions.'

Layard's observations betray a similar discomfort and embarrassment to that suggested by Spielmann. Both obviously knew more, but settled for discretion . . .

What happened between the Oval Test of August 1882, which gave rise to the myth of the Ashes, and their emergence as a reality on the other side of the world six months later, has become shrouded in mystery in its telling, and lack of telling, down the years.

Explanatory attempts by MCC and *Wisden* tend to confuse the various aspects rather than clarify them. Since 1954, *Wisden* has said it all — in a fashion:

'The Ashes were originated in 1882 when, on 29 August, Australia defeated the full strength of England on English soil for the first time. The Australians won by the narrow margin of seven runs and the following day, the *Sporting Times* printed a mock obituary notice, written by Shirley Brooks, son of an editor of *Punch*, which read: "In affectionate remembrance of English cricket which died at The Oval, 29th August 1882. Deeply lamented by a large circle of sorrowing friends and acquaintances. R.I.P. N.B.: The body will be cremated and the Ashes taken to Australia."

'The following winter, the Hon. Ivo Bligh, afterwards Lord Darnley, set out to Australia to recover these mythical Ashes. Australia won the first match by nine wickets, but England won the next two, and the real Ashes came into being when some Melbourne women burnt a bail used in the third game and presented the ashes in an urn to Ivo Bligh.

'When Lord Darnley died in 1927, the urn, by a bequest in his will, was given to MCC, and it held a place of honour in the Long Room at Lord's until 1953 when, with other cricket treasures, it was moved to the newly-built Imperial Cricket Memorial near the pavilion. There it stands permanently, together with the velvet bag in which the urn was originally given to Lord Darnley and the score card of the 1882 match.'

Not a word of this explanation has been altered since it was first published in 1954. *Wisden* is supported by MCC in its pamphlet, *The Story of the Ashes*:

'. . . It had been commonly said that Ivo Bligh had gone on a pilgrimage to "recover the Ashes", and so, after the second defeat of Murdoch's team, some Melbourne ladies collected the ashes of a bail, which they placed in a small pottery urn and presented to him. One of the donors was a Miss Florence Rose Morphy, the future Mrs Ivo Bligh. An additional gift, made by a Mrs J. W. Fletcher, was a red velvet bag to contain the ashes. Both the urn and the bag were personal gifts which Lord Darnley treasured until his death, when his widow, the former Miss Morphy, sent them to Lord's for safekeeping. Thus the urn never changes hands, and when England and Australia play against each other in a Test series for "the Ashes", there is no trophy either given or received . . .'

13

Wisden ignores Florence Morphy while MCC does little more than acknowledge her existence, and the majority of other authorities seem to fall back on either *Wisden* or MCC. *Debrett's Peerage*, however, reveals that she was the daughter of the late Stephen Morphy, of Beechworth, Victoria, Australia.

European explorers, pushing doggedly into the north-east of Victoria in the early 1820s, were the first outsiders to travel through the Ovens River valley. Some fifteen years later, in May 1839, a settler called Reid, who wished to extend his holdings, found a range of hills which was besieged by a riot of colours both then and in the autumn. He called the site May Day Hills.

Florence, Countess of Darnley

In the quiet birth of this settlement, there was no hint of its hectic youth in store. When a Victorian Government surveyor arrived, he was reminded of his home town in Leicestershire, England, so May Day Hills was put on the map as Beechworth. The name has endured.

The pulse of the little settlement, normally so steady, went wild in 1851 when a prospecting party found gold and consequently changed the rhythm of history for the whole of the Ovens region. The bush telegraph hummed; and the current sent a vision of instant wealth through 2000 Chinese immigrants scattered along the eastern seaboard of Australia. They dropped whatever they happened to be doing, flung their possessions into wheel-

14

barrows, and made a push for the outback. From clouds of dust and flies issued the bewildered squeals of pigs. The Chinese drove or dragged their swine everywhere with them.

The gold fever was also caught by many Europeans and even by some Americans. Propelled by the shimmering halo over Beechworth, they uprooted themselves and took to the trail. This was a choking hell in summer and a squelching quagmire in winter. The creaking of punished wheels intermingled with the lowing of plodding bullock teams which were constantly being overtaken by the scurrying Chinese.

The first encounter with the harsh reality of the outback must have caused many a step to falter. The journey from Melbourne to the Ovens took at best

John Stephen Morphy

three weeks, but Beechworth's population nevertheless soared during a few months from several hundred to about 10 000.

A simple, hard-working community was transformed into something like a refugee camp. A hot curry of humanity with a pathetically inadequate support system became sprawled over a great octopus of wounded land. These goldfields, during their heyday in the 1850s and 1860s, attracted between 30 000 and 40 000 people.

When the diggers arrived, they split instinctively into two groups, labelled Punchers and Monkeys. The Punchers were 'dry', working the banks and gullys, while the Monkeys were 'wet', labouring in the streams. Away from

15

The site in Havelock Road, Beechworth, Victoria, where the eighth Countess of Darnley was born

their picks, shovels, and pans, they retained distinctive appearances. The Monkeys wore black woollen trousers, silk sashes, Napoleon boots, and a superiority complex. The Punchers were less flamboyant and theatrical, usually in moleskin trousers. Almost everybody carried a gun, and the police were never idle for long.

As the precious metal poured into Beechworth, it created an urgent need for a resident State Government official to buy the gold and organise transport for its long and hazardous journey to the Treasury in Melbourne. The Government turned to a shrewd and level-headed Irish immigrant called John Stephen Morphy and appointed him mining warden and gold com-

The hearse used for the funeral of John Morphy in Beechworth, Victoria

missioner. Mr Morphy, a family man, had previously spent seventeen years in New South Wales, having arrived in Sydney from Killarney, County Kerry, where his ancestors had sprung from royalty. His wife, formerly Elizabeth Ann Styles, born in Sydney, was of Kent stock.

The courageous Morphys, with their expanding brood, established themselves about a kilometre east of the centre of Beechworth in a slab and bark house on a few hectares approached by a dirt track which was eventually to be named Havelock Road. The property also had some outbuildings, including stables.

John Morphy's job was a formidable challenge. He had to issue mining

17

licences — the law required that these should be renewed each month — settle disputes and make judgements on minor criminal charges. At first, he had the help of only three policemen, who, like the diggers, lived in tents.

The law also demanded clean and orderly tents. The tents of the Chinese were often filthy; also their pigs frequently went on the rampage. Neither were the Orientals above theft. They appeared before Morphy in his capacity as mining warden and once he fined a Chinese ten shillings for cutting out and stealing the pocket of a compatriot.

About the time that his seventh and last child, a daughter called Florence Rose, was born in August 1860, Morphy took on the additional job of police magistrate. At first in his court room, he was forced to use equipment from the commissioner's office because the Government officials in Melbourne had forgotten to arrange delivery of the necessary furniture and stationery.

It had been recognised for some time in Beechworth that John Morphy was overworked. The district needed an additional gold commissioner and requests had been made for one, but nothing had come of these when, on 13 July 1861, Morphy died suddenly of apoplexy. Over the years, he had won much respect — especially among his fellow officials — and his unexpected death came as a big shock to the community. Many tradespeople closed for the day of his funeral and hundreds joined in the procession behind the impressive horse-drawn hearse, its highly polished black bodywork reflecting stabs of harsh sunlight as it progressed with solemnity to the Roman Catholic section of Beechworth Cemetery, to a graveside within sight of the Chinese burning towers.

Magistrate Morphy left a widow with seven children, the youngest of whom, Florence, was not quite eleven months old. The family continued to live for several more years in the Beechworth district, but changed homes and rented their original house. A government pension was eventually arranged for Mrs Morphy and with this, rents from Havelock Road and another property behind the Town Hall, and perhaps contributions from her older working sons, she was able to keep poverty at bay. Later, the family moved into the Melbourne suburb of Hawthorne.

As the younger Morphys, Lucy, Kate, and Florence, grew, it became increasingly obvious that the 'baby' of the family, Florence, was extremely intelligent and versatile; also her exceptional looks and natural charm began to turn heads and halt conversations. These attributes, allied with a sound education and grounding in the social graces, won her access to wealthy and influential circles. In 1881, aged twenty-one, she emerged as a member of the retinue of William Clarke, the immensely-rich head of the Clarke clan in Victoria. Florence had secured the post of music teacher to the Clarke children and companion to Mr Clarke's wife, Janet, at the family's country mansion, Rupertswood, in Sunbury, some 50 kilometres from Melbourne.

On the morning of 13 September 1881, William Clarke's party went aboard the SS *Bokhara* anchored at Williamstoun Pier in Melbourne and began the long voyage to England. The travellers had no idea that the return journey, a year hence on the SS *Peshawur*, would be as hazardous—and for young Florence Morphy as momentous—as the pioneering voyage was from London to Tasmania in 1829 of William's father, William John Turner 'Big' Clarke.

CHAPTER 2

Charles Dickens would doubtless have enjoyed unravelling the truth about the mystery-shrouded Ashes and the colourful people, rich and poor, carefree and burdened, who chanced to be involved in their creation. Dickens probably met two of the chief characters when they were still children, but the great novelist died in 1870—twelve years before the action started with the Oval Test of 1882.

The Oval, 1880, and the English captain, Lord Harris, chases to prevent a boundary during the first Test match

This Test was only the second between England and Australia to be played in England. The first had also been played at The Oval, two years previously, on 6, 7 and 8 September, England winning by five wickets. This second Oval Test was also to become recognised as the ninth Test between the two countries, although the term 'Test' was not used in a cricketing context and officially recognised as such until some years later.

By the time they arrived at The Oval on 28 August 1882, the touring Australians had already played twenty-nine matches at venues throughout Britain ranging from Portsmouth to Edinburgh. Of these, they had won eighteen, drawn eight, and lost three. The defeats had been at the hands of Cambridge, the Players of England, and Past and Present of Cambridge University. The Test was the visitors' fourth match of the tour at Kennington Oval. Here, in May, they had beaten Surrey by six wickets, in June beaten the Gentlemen of England by an innings and a run, and lost earlier in August to the Players by an innings and 34 runs. Their ambition now, as in 1880, was to beat All-England for the first time on English soil.

But the tourists had some problems. The right-handed batsman, Percy McDonnell, had an injury which put him out of the reckoning; and George Palmer, a fine medium-pace bowler, was suffering from muscle strain. A session in the nets ended somewhat indecisively for him and, finally, he was excluded from the side on medical advice.

Consequently, the team chosen was: Alexander Chalmers Bannerman (batsman, New South Wales), John McCarthy Blackham (wicket-keeper, Victoria), George Bonnor (batsman, Victoria and New South Wales), Henry Frederick Boyle, (bowler, Victoria), Thomas William Garrett (bowler, New South Wales), George Giffen (all-rounder, South Australia), Thomas Patrick Horan (batsman, Victoria), Samuel Percy Jones (batsman, New South Wales), Hugh Hamon Massie (batsman, New South Wales), William Lloyd Murdoch (captain, and batsman rated only second to Grace; New South Wales and Sussex), and Frederick Robert Spofforth (fast bowler extraordinary, New South Wales, Victoria, and Derbyshire).

The Australian touring team in England in 1882. Standing, from left: G. E. Palmer, H. F. Boyle, W. L. Murdoch (capt.), P. S. McDonnell, F. R. Spofforth, T. P. Horan, S. P. Jones. Seated, from left: C. W. Beal (manager), G. Giffen, A. C. Bannerman, T. W. Garrett, H. H. Massie, and G. J. Bonnor

The England team was selected by Lord Harris, Mr I. D. Walker, Mr V. E. Walker and the former secretary of the Surrey County Cricket Club, Mr F. Burbridge.

The only first-choice player not available was the Nottinghamshire fast bowler, Frederick Morley, who was ill. The next choice was the Lancashire batsman and captain, Albert Neilson Hornby, who was also appointed captain for the Test. The rest of the team was Richard Gorton Barlow (all-rounder, Lancashire), William Barnes (all-rounder, Nottinghamshire), Doctor William Gilbert Grace (master batsman, Gloucestershire), Alfred Perry Lucas

Umpire Robert Thoms

(batsman, Cambridge University, Surrey, Middlesex and Essex), Alfred Lyttelton (wicket-keeper, Cambridge and Middlesex), Allan Gibson Steel (all-rounder, Lancashire), Charles Thomas Studd (all-rounder, Cambridge and Middlesex), Edmund Peate (bowler, Yorkshire), John Maurice Read (all-rounder, Surrey), and George Ulyett (bowler, Yorkshire). Umpires were R. Thoms and L. Greenwood.

It had been a miserably wet weekend in London and the Monday morning of 28 August, although sultry, offered little prospect of any sun. More rain seemed a distinct possibility. Cloud rolled low and dark across The Oval, but the clicking turnstiles indicated that the capital's cricket lovers were not easily deterred. All the seats were soon occupied and the standing space quickly began to fill.

In the pavilion, shortly before noon, Hornby spun a coin. Murdoch called and won. Both captains had, of course, inspected the wicket. This was patchy from overwork. Earlier in August, it had been alternately soaked and baked, and over the two days immediately before the match had been made sodden again. With little encouragement, it would start breaking up—and the immediate prospect for it was a three-day pounding. Settling, hopefully, for the lesser of two evils, Murdoch decided to bat.

No sooner had the twelve strokes of Big Ben floated across the Thames than the England side emerged to applause from around the packed ground. The fielding side was followed almost immediately by the Australian openers, Alexander Chalmers Bannerman and Hugh Hamon Massie.

The name of Bannerman had already been made secure in Test cricket history by Charles, the elder brother of Alec, who was the first to make a Test century—in the first Test, at Melbourne, in 1877 when he made 165 before retiring hurt. The Bannermans were originally from Kent.

Massie, an attacking right-hand batsman, had started the tour sensationally

An aerial photograph of The Oval taken during the 1970s

23

by scoring 206 in three hours at Oxford, his fiery second hundred of this coming while his partners scored only 12.

Now the applause at The Oval gave way to a babble of excited speculation as the batsmen took their bearings. The slow left-hand spinner, Peate, measured out his run from the gasometer end and went through the motions of a delivery.

For Peate, Lyttelton was standing close at the wicket, Grace at point, Steel at slip, Barlow at long slip, Hornby forward short-leg, Barnes at long-on, Read at long-off, Studd at mid-off, Ulyett at third man, and Lucas at cover point.

At 12.10, Bannerman, shaping up for first strike, and Peate moving in, silenced the crowd.

After treating the first airy deliveries with lavish respect, Bannerman drove the slightly over-pitched last ball of the four-ball over into the covers for 3. Lucas, with centimetres to spare, prevented the first boundary.

The all-Yorkshire attack was now taken up by Ulyett from the pavilion end. For the paceman, Lyttelton moved back a few steps, Grace was at point, Steel at slip, Peate at long slip, Barnes third man, Studd cover point, Barlow mid-off, Hornby mid-on, Lucas short-leg, and Read long-leg. Bannerman retained the strike and a maiden ensued. And so Massie came to face Peate who quickly found line and length. Far from comfortable, Massie was restricted to a single in the direction of long-on.

In Ulyett's next over, there was a bye and Bannerman cut him for a single.

Peate, by now, was almost hanging the ball on the moist air, but Bannerman was not tempted.

Massie, betraying impatience, was badly beaten in trying to force Ulyett; he went for the next one, too: it was straight, of fuller length. A shout went up as Massie's leg stump went. So much for the double-century maker. First blood to England — Australia one for 6.

Murdoch came in and, without brooding, the Australian skipper square cut Ulyett along the ground for 4 — the first boundary of the day. The manner of execution reminded some who watched of Murdoch's performance here two years previously when the bearded leader scored 153 — pipping Grace by one for the highest score of that match. But now, on a wicket that he quickly realised was bent on villainy, Murdoch reined in.

Bannerman, for all his caution, eventually edged Peate down the leg side — and gleaned 2 lucky runs.

Virtually nothing was evading Grace at point. Applause broke out twice as he denied the batsmen. Murdoch eventually worked Ulyett away on the leg side for 2 and, soon afterwards, for 2 more. Some minutes later, he drove the paceman to long-on for another couple, thus reaching 10.

When the total reached 18, Hornby made his first bowling change, replacing Ulyett with Barlow's medium pace.

Bannerman took advantage of Barlow's settling in to move along from 4. He managed a couple of neat singles. His captain did likewise. But now the

England v. Australia, Kennington Oval, 1882

flow of runs was halted as each batsman, try as he might, became bogged down. With each over, the fielding tightened and it seemed at times as though even the rare aggressive stroke was aimed at a fielder.

Peate and Barlow toiled relentlessly through fourteen successive maidens. A single to Murdoch was the sole harvest from seventeen overs.

Something had to give, and eventually it did in somewhat surprising fashion. Murdoch, in attempting to force away Peate, turned the ball on to his own stumps.

The crowd, patience rewarded, roared for the second time and heads turned to the scoreboard — two for 21.

Searching eyes picked out the Australian Hercules and cheers rang out as Bonnor took calm strides over the turf. Of him, the crowd expected much the same as we do today of Ian Botham and the less predictable Rodney Marsh. Expectations were reflected in the field as Hornby spread out his men for the big hitter.

Peate bowled to him and agonisingly beat the bat. Bonnor survived to tuck away the next delivery for a single. Now he prepared to face Barlow's offerings. In fact, only one offering was necessary: this kept low and took out his middle stump.

Three for 22 after an hour of play. Bannerman awaited his fourth partner. This was Horan, a reliable defender and currently the best batsmen in Victoria, but the next runs came from the surviving opener.

Bannerman advanced to 9 by late-cutting Barlow for 3 and thereby came up against Peate again. Perhaps he was deceived by the movement through the air. The resulting chance was hard and to any other part of the field might have yielded runs, but it sped low above the turf slightly backward of point to be intercepted by the cat-like Grace who made a difficult catch look

25

relatively easy. Australia's safest-looking batsman of the morning departed, angry with himself for his lapse. His team was in trouble.

Horan, still looking for that first run, was joined by Giffen. Their task was formidable, Peate and Barlow, who already seemed assured of tomorrow's tall stories, allowed neither of the new batsmen respite. Both managed to contribute to the Australian tally, but only marginally. Horan made a shaky 3 before his leg stump went to the now rampant Barlow; and Giffen, with a single to his credit, was clean bowled by the mesmerising Peate — six for 30.

In the pavilion, Murdoch silently castigated himself for having elected to bat first and third. His 13 was the highest score so far. At this rate, they would be lucky to manage a total of 50. He couldn't know it then, but Blackham and Garrett were starting on the biggest partnership of the innings — and Garrett a fast bowler!

From each end, Garrett made an on-drive for 2, and after 100 minutes of tense play, Australia reached 40. It seemed to have taken an eternity. Bowling changes were made. Ulyett resumed at the pavilion end and Peate was rested in favour of Steel. Each of them bowled two overs before, as *The Times* put it, luncheon was announced.

Blackham and Garrett had survived the session. Blackham was on 3 and Garrett 10. Peate and Barlow each recorded twenty maidens, yet not a minute of the play had been dull.

After lunch, Peate, who had come a long way in cricket since first playing in a circus troupe, again took up his role from under the gasometer. The wily Yorkshireman made the final delivery of his first over irresistibly teasing to Garrett, who swung mightily and connected with the meat of his bat. However, the trajectory was not quite as high as he had hoped and Read moved easily to take a comfortable catch at long-off. This seventh wicket stand had put on 18, but Australia was still two short of 50 and had only three wickets in hand.

Boyle took his guard and faced Barlow. The first delivery he fended off clumsily, the ball falling just short of Hornby's clutching hands at mid-on. In the next three overs, he managed to scramble a couple of singles, the first of these bringing up the 50. Then Barlow sent his bails spinning — eight for 51.

Thus twenty-one-year-old Jones, the baby of the Australian side, came to the wicket for his Test debut in England.

Before taking the strike, he watched the old-hand, Blackham, cut Peate into the encroaching spectators for only the second boundary of the day. A few minutes later, Blackham chalked up the third boundary when he drove straight. Jones, meanwhile, had to be content with pushing forward and repeatedly seeing the ball swooped on by Hornby in close attendance.

Renewing his duel with Barlow, Blackham stepped back to a short delivery which kept lower than he expected. The ball arced against the clouds and fell in the neighbourhood of point where it was nonchalantly accepted by Grace — nine for 59 of which Blackham had made the most with 17.

William Grace

Australia's last man, Spofforth, came to the crease. With his only scoring stroke, he drove Peate for the fourth boundary.

Jones, still seeking his first run, swung frustratedly at Barlow. He recovered his balance just in time to see Barnes bag the ball at third man. It was the only duck of the innings.

The Australians were all out for 63 — their lowest total of the tour.

A horse pulling a roller was urged on to the field as the players left.

The heroes of the hour were Barlow and Peate. Barlow had bowled 31 overs, of which 22 were maidens, and taken five wickets for 19 runs. Peate had bowled 38, of which 24 were maidens, and taken four wickets for 31.

At 3.30, Barlow and Grace opened for England. The Australian attack was spearheaded by Spofforth from the gasometer end. His field was: Blackham standing back, Garrett cover point, Jones long slip, Boyle short mid-on, Murdoch point, Bannerman short mid-off, Bonnor slip, Horan forward short-leg, Giffen long-on, and Massie long-off.

Spofforth's first delivery was short. It sizzled at little more than bail height past Barlow's bat and off stump, and eluded Blackham's plunge. The batsmen crossed twice and 4 byes were narrowly averted. Barlow clipped the next delivery off his legs forward of square for England's first run.

From his position behind the stumps to take Spofforth, Blackham moved forward half the distance for Garrett, the other prong of the Australian opening attack. Spofforth went to mid-on, Jones long slip, Boyle short mid-on, Murdoch point, Bannerman mid-off, Bonnor slip, Horan short-leg, Giffen long-off, and Massie cover point.

Garrett lacked the pace of Spofforth, but was immediately straighter and his first effort almost had Barlow playing on. After such a close shave, the Lancastrian was glad to adopt a defensive attitude. A maiden over to Garrett.

Garrett's next over, to Grace, was also a maiden. Between these, Grace took a single to the off from Spofforth. Garrett's third over, however, cost 6 runs: Grace snatched another single; and Barlow put him away to leg for 2, and then 3.

Grace took another single off Spofforth and so did Barlow, who then negotiated another maiden with Garrett.

The changeover pitted the Demon against the fortress that was Grace. WG pushed a single to the off. Massie scooped up. Barlow took a similar liberty. Facing Garrett again, Barlow gained in confidence and drove hard to beat Boyle at mid-on — 3 more. Grace picked off another single to put himself in Spofforth's sights again.

Perhaps the yorker deceived Grace by gaining some movement through the air. Whatever . . . the master batsman lost the line and his leg stump — England one for 13.

Grace's contribution of 4 was to vanish without trace in his awesome career figures.

George Ulyett was next to the wicket, making up a Yorkshire–Lancashire

28

How an artist from the *Illustrated Sporting and Dramatic News* saw the action at The Oval with Spofforth bowling to Grace. The umpire is Bob Thoms

alliance for the common good. Before scoring, the Yorkshireman gave a stumping chance which was missed by Blackham. Could Ulyett now make good his second life? Five runs later, he was unnerved again by seeing Barlow snapped up brilliantly by the darting Bannerman at mid-off. Spofforth has his second victim — England two for 18.

Ulyett was joined by Lucas, an instinctively defensive batsman and usually a steadying influence. He watched Ulyett drive Garrett for an authorative 4 and then concentrated on Spofforth.

Spurred on by his success, the Demon let fly down the wild side and, to his chagrin, saw the ball travel for 4 byes. Neither was Blackham able to gather the next delivery cleanly . . . another bye.

Spofforth then aimed for the leg stump. The ball was fractionally short and Lucas moved swiftly, sweeping to leg and opening his account with a well-placed boundary.

Forty came up in fifty minutes and, after another single, Murdoch made his first bowling change. Boyle took up the initiative from the gasometer end and Spofforth tried the other direction. The 50 came up in just under an hour, due mainly to some free hitting by Ulyett. Brilliant fielding by Murdoch at point often brought applause. Ulyett put Spofforth away powerfully to leg for 3, but soon after this, went down the wicket, swinging recklessly, and was stumped by Blackham who had time to spare — England three for 57.

Ulyett, with his dashing 26, was the highest scorer so far.

Lyttelton, a right-hander and one of eight cricketing brothers, was next to the crease. For half an hour, there was a calm which yielded only 3 runs.

Eventually, Lucas, in trying to force Boyle, gave an edge which was

29

snapped up by Blackham. Lucas had taken a long time over his 9 and merited more—four for 59.

Studd was the new man with the double of 1000 runs and 100 wickets for the season under his belt. The crowd expected runs from him. Would Studd oblige?

Boyle moved in to test the Cambridge man—who groped forward and was badly beaten by a short ball that shot past very low. Studd eyed first the pitch and then the thick clouds. The gloom was not encouraging.

Spofforth thundered in again and Lyttelton tried to drive to the off, but got only an edge which went to leg with Horan like a ferret after it.

The batsmen crossed for Studd to face the music again. Spofforth hit full stride and throttle. The ball pitched outside the off stump, biting and turning sharply. Too late, Studd dabbed at air as the bails and stumps parted company—five for 60.

George Ulyett

Read saw out the over, taking a single off the last ball to retain the strike. He took 2 off the next to put England level with the Australian total. Fifty minutes of play remained before stumps.

The totals were still level when Spofforth fired in. Lyttelton was caught flat-footed. Many spectators lost sight of the ball until Blackham, appealing for a catch, held it aloft—six for 63.

Barnes reached the crease and took advice on his security from the umpire. The tall right-hander immediately notched a single with a rather untidy cover drive and in the next over, disturbed spectators who were spilling onto the field at square leg.

Spofforth, in his next over, made one climb again to rap Read in the ribs.

Soon after this, England reached 70. It was 5.20. The gloom persisted. Read was hit again by Spofforth — this time on a knee; and then on an elbow by the Demon. Hardly had Read recovered from these knocks than Boyle made one turn very late to skittle Barnes who had made five — seven for 70.

Suddenly, the gloom of the crowd matched the skies.

Steel came out, hoping to be able to restore the fortunes of England, and soon hit the ball for 2. After two hours' hard work, England had made 75. What sort of a lead could they establish before stumps?

Read, bruised but far from broken, launched into a revival by late-cutting Boyle through the slips for 3. And the crowd was fully alive again when he drove Spofforth to leg for 4. Steel joined in the offensive, too. He thrashed Boyle and spectators scrambled out of the way as big Bonnor thundered towards them and retrieved just inside the boundary. They were too excited to squat again until shouted down by people behind; and leapt up once more as Steel hit Spofforth. Another 3.

Something in the air, in the clouds, suggested the spree would be short-lived. Murdoch tuned in and brought back the long-rested Garrett for Boyle. England, by now, was on 88 and in the driving seat. Boyle's second delivery was clouted by Steel safely beyond reach of Murdoch for another boundary. Read gave another section of spectators some exercise as he dealt out more punishment to Spofforth.

Murdoch kept his cool. Boyle moved in again. The ball went well wide, but Steel got an inside edge and dragged it on to his stumps.

Eight for 96. The partnership, second best of the innings, had put on 26 and revived the 20 000 crowd packing The Oval. The cheers accompanying Hornby to the middle were renewed when Read hammered Spofforth for 3 to put England on 99.

Ten minutes before stumps, it was the skipper, Hornby, who appropriately brought up the 100 with a single off Spofforth. He managed to push another single before losing his leg stump to a fiery shooter from the Demon — nine for 101.

The last man, Peate, groped at a scorcher and the ball flew low to be taken easily by Boyle at short mid-off.

Spofforth's seven for 46 put all other performances in the shade. England faced the second day with a first innings lead of 38 and for this modest advantage, England were indebted to two batsmen in particular: Ulyett for his swashbuckling 26 and the unbeaten and polished 19 from Read.

During the night, the fitful August weather turned wet and cold. Windows wept. Soot collapsed on dead cinders. Daylight brought sneaky showers which became a downpour by ten. Pessimists saw dancing splashes, rubbish afloat in gutters, and wrote off any chance of cricket.

Optimists who had seen twenty Test wickets fall the previous day, struggled prematurely into winter topcoats and headed for The Oval. Umbrellas blossomed like prosperous fungus farms outside each entrance to the cricket ground long before the turnstiles began clicking again.

From the left: R. Pilling, A. Watson and 'O, my Hornby and my Barlow long ago!'

About 11 a.m. the clouds began to break up, the rain fizzled out, and the light improved. The ground, of course, was still soaking and play, scheduled to start at 11.30, was delayed until 12.10. Even as the players came out, some observers thought the ground still unfit.

Debate over this continued as Barlow, from the pavilion end, engaged Bannerman. The wiry little opener from New South Wales promptly drove into the covers for 2, but he retreated into a shell for the rest of the over as the Lancashire paceman found line and length.

Ulyett, operating at the gasometer end, introduced himself with a loosener. Massie, ignoring pleasantries, thundered him through the covers. Four runs seemed assured—until Read flashed round to stop the ball within centimetres of the boundary rope. Three runs. Bannerman, with neat but unproductive strokes, saw out the over.

Against Barlow, Massie maintained his belligerence and soon had the crowd in a permanent state of excitement. Grace stretched in vain for a stroke over point and before he recovered, the ball leapt the rope. There was a scramble of young enthusiasts to return it.

Barlow went for the leg stump. Brimming with confidence, Massie read him and swept. The resulting sound was not the firm rap of bat meeting ball, but the smack of wet leather being trapped between the wicket-keeper's gloves. Massie's next scoring stroke was wide of point to glean a single.

The field changed over for Ulyett who toiled in and put all his Yorkshire swarthiness into the effort. Massie went forward powerfully to the pitch but met nothing. Inexplicably, the stumps remained intact. Lyttelton collected very low. After that, the batsman was glad merely to hold his ground for a while.

Barlow allowed Bannerman only to consolidate his reputation as a stone-waller and each batsman contributed just a single before Ulyett again had the adventurous Massie groping and beaten.

More singles, mostly from Massie, pushed the score along to 25 when Hornby decided on a bowling change. Peate relieved his county colleague and began with a maiden—to the impassive Bannerman, of course. Barlow then gave way to Studd whose bowling had not been called on the previous day. Massie, it seemed, had been waiting for Studd and drove the first delivery for 4 to the corner of the stand in front of the Tavern. He fenced at the next two with an experimental air—then smashed the fourth straight with wincing force. Most eyes followed the action through to the long-on boundary. Here they became stranded momentarily before obliged to back-track. Delayed applause burst from all sides as it dawned that Studd had stopped the unstoppable, rocking the Victorian batsman on his heels. It was easily the best bit of cricket so far. The bowler tossed the ball away, walked to his fielding position, and nursed his fingers throughout the next over.

Massie reflected on the boundary that might have been but his next two scoring strokes, both off Peate, wiped off the arrears for the Australians. He took another single off Peate and then stamped his authority by gloriously

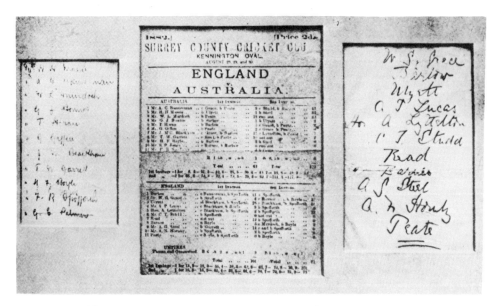

The scorecard and the captains' batting lists for the Oval Test, 1882

driving Studd to leg and over the ropes.

Next, Bannerman reminded everybody he was still there by twice cutting Peate for 2.

At 47 without loss, Barnes was brought into the attack. Massie, on 38 by this time, lofted his first ball hopefully for 6, but it plummeted short. Lucas, at long-on in front of the pavilion, steadied himself to take the catch. The ball went straight through his hands. The crowd sent up a cry of anguish. Thus Massie began his second life, playing out with paradoxical defensiveness the next three deliveries.

Two more were needed for the 50. Bannerman secured these by cutting Peate for 2.

Peate was in line for more punishment and Massie, the executioner, hit him to the long-on boundary and then almost straight for 2. To stem the flow, Hornby brought on Steel and put Ulyett and Grace in close attendance to the second-fiddle Bannerman who continued in neat defiance.

A single and a couple brought up Massie's personal 50 and the crowd was unstinting in its appreciation of the first batting performance to complement the bowling feat of Spofforth the previous day. Massie celebrated by hitting Steel to square leg for 4, but, in his next over, Steel had the final say in that particular dispute by uprooting Massie's leg stump. The opener—with nine 4s, two 3s, and three 2s—had made 55 out of 66 in about an hour but Hornby had achieved the breakthrough.

The spreading field stirred the crowd as Bonnor joined Bannerman. Steel ran in again and there was a gasp from all sides as he made the big man push at air. However, Bonnor middled the next for 2.

Now Hornby surprised everyone. Steel had accomplished the breakthrough, yet he was taken off in favour of Ulyett. There were even a few boos, perhaps from supporters of Lancashire, but Ulyett ignored them. Gingerly, Bonnor fended off the first three deliveries, but the fourth and fastest efficiently extracted his middle stump. Those who had booed promptly forgave Hornby and joined the cheering.

Next to join Bannerman was Murdoch. The Australian captain was applauded all the way to the centre. Before taking strike, however, he watched the surviving opener caught at extra mid-off by Studd off Barnes — three for 70. Bannerman had made a careful, almost unnoticed, 13 in seventy minutes.

There was a babble of speculation as Horan appeared, vigorously hoping to improve on his first innings tally of 3. With Murdoch, he set about the vital task of re-establishing the Australian innings.

Bent on preventing this, Hornby again switched bowlers. No boos this time as Peate replaced Ulyett. Some singles came — six to Murdoch, two to Horan.

Ted Peate

As the tempo settled again, a few spectators with a weather eye pointed at the darkly banking clouds, shivered, and returned their attention to the green battlefield.

They saw Peate produce an almost lazily-loose delivery — which Horan obligingly lifted to point, giving Grace one of the simplest catches imaginable. Horan left the field as baffled by the manner of his dismissal as any of the 20 000 who watched it — four for 79.

Giffen, on emerging, hoped that Horan might offer a word of advice in passing, but there was none. Giffen took guard, looked around the field suspiciously, then concentrated on Peate. The batsman stretched forward, low, felt the contact—and in virtually the same moment became aghast as Grace, his beard flowing on the wind, jubilantly held up the ball. The disbelieving crowd erupted—five for 79.

Peate was on a hat-trick. Murdoch sought consolation in leaning on his bat as he watched the dependable Jack Blackham approach. Would the wicket-keeper stay with him? Murdoch shifted his weight as Peate jogged in again.

The spell hung as the Yorkshireman elected for a long-hop and yet again the crowd bellowed—but this time for a boundary belted by Blackham to put him immediately among the runs. Momentarily, Murdoch let himself relax.

Still feeling high, Peate let a measure of philosophy direct the final delivery of this eventful over, and Blackham was wily enough to adopt a similar response.

Australia, with five wickets to fall, was 45 ahead. Had Peate any more surprises up his sleeve? From the first ball of his next over, Blackham got an edge. Before the crowd could react, the ball had dropped just short of Steel at slip. Quelling his alarm, Blackham scrambled a single.

At the expense of the spinner, Murdoch took 2 from each of the next two deliveries and, in this manner, the Australian total reached 90. Four byes now put the tourists well into the 90s, but only from a cleverly-flighted delivery which completely beat the Australian skipper and perhaps scratched the varnish on his stumps. Again the crowd buzzed.

Barnes took up the issue with Blackham who forced a single. As umbrellas began sprouting again, Murdoch drove with gusto into the covers for 3.

The first spots of rain suddenly developed into heavy curtains driving across the field. The moment the ball was dead, the players dashed for shelter, funnelling into the pavilion. It was 1.50. Lunch was taken a few minutes earlier than scheduled.

The downpour was brief and play was resumed on time at 2.45. But what had yet another soaking done to the pitch? Peate would try to find the answer. And amid the uncertainty, Blackham began the task of settling in again.

He dealt safely enough with the first three deliveries, each of which left its fading impression on the pitch. A maiden loomed as Peate released the last ball—to have it nudged by the devil for an edge. Lyttelton made a neat job of the catch at the wicket to give Peate a maiden wicket—six for 99.

Anxious to make amends for his first-innings duck and improve the prospects for his Test career, young Jones came to the support of his captain. Before getting the strike, however, he had to watch Murdoch cope with Barlow who was operating from the pavilion. Devastating with the ball the previous day, the Lancastrian today was still looking for his first wicket. Would these conditions favour or deny him?

Murdoch found a gap which earned a single and put up the 100—a target struggled for all the way since the departure of marauding Massie.

Jones, then, took his guard and concentrated fiercely on narrowing his world to the belligerent and rapidly-approaching figure of Barlow. The delivery was fractionally short and lifted obligingly. Jones made to cut, avoided an edge more by good luck than good management and thereby made the first 2, in England, of his 432 runs in twelve Test matches.

His next stroke, to a ball lifting in similar fashion, was timed with a sweetness more worthy of his skill and Jones consequently chalked up his first boundary. The crowd demonstrated its charity and Jones flushed with youthful pride. The colour drained from his cheeks as quickly as it sprang, subject to a silent disciplinarian within. There was still a daunting job ahead of him.

Sammy Jones

From the start, the youngster was confounded by Peate. The Yorkshire destroyer was getting less from the air than on the previous day, but his varying pace and turn repeatedly deceived Jones who was reduced to nudging and padding, to prodding at patches of turf and to scratching his head. Consolation eluded him.

Murdoch, fully occupied with problems of his own, at last forced 2 more from Barlow, and Jones again confronted his tormentor. Runs became as scarce as chickens' teeth. Hunched against the chilling wind from the river, the clergymen dotted among the spectators drew comfort from their cigars. These glowed with fervour when Murdoch eventually drove Barlow into the covers for an easy enough single, then rashly decided there was 2 for the taking.

There was a shout. The ball became a blur. Bails jumped. Appeals rang out as Jones flew beyond the stumps. The umpire decided in favour of the batsman. The breeze quickly dispersed cigar-smoke signals and lifted the odd flake of ash from a coat lapel.

With the total at 113, Barlow was rested and Steel came back, Hornby thus unwittingly setting the scene for the incident which, more than any other factor, was attributed with lifting this Test match from merely fine entertainment to that of classic status worth recalling 100 years later.

Murdoch, embattled to a degree comparable with the plight of his younger partner, despatched Steel dangerously fine on the off and not in any way the direction he intended. Lyttelton clawed in vain, a single was accrued. Jones, considering the ball dead and himself safely home, went back along the pitch to service, in his fashion, an irregularity, real or imagined. As he thumped the offending area with the bottom of his bat, he was attracted by the sound of rattling bails, coupled with an appeal from Grace standing over the stumps.

Jones switched his startled gaze to umpire Robert Thoms standing in bulky and inscrutable contemplation. A procession of bad-tempered clouds chased across The Oval as Thoms lifted the finger of doom.

Flushing again, this time in anger, Jones hesitated only to glance at his skipper. Murdoch watched everything impassively. Jones began walking, turning twice during his exit to glare with eyes like blowlamps in the direction of Grace.

Suddenly, all the other England players discovered crises of personal minutia to consume their attention, be it tying laces, blowing noses, or pulling up socks — seven for 114.

Enter Spofforth, with bat, to watch first Murdoch take 3 off Peate. Without advantage going either way, Spofforth saw his way through an over from Steel.

Murdoch next struck a single from Peate to put Spofforth on the spot again. The Demon fended away the first delivery, but went across the second which left him momentarily studying the new angles adopted by his leg and middle stump. He walked back briskly in the direction from which he had but recently approached the centre — eight for 117.

Soon after Garrett reached the wicket, Murdoch defiantly heaved Steel high and straight, but Ulyett, moving swiftly round the boundary, gathered and returned quickly to save 3 runs. Murdoch made 2 more by off-driving Peate.

Garrett eventually forced Steel into the covers for 2. It was Hornby who gathered the ball and Murdoch, remembering an arm injury sustained by Hornby, reckoned there was a third for the taking. He started down the pitch — to waver at Garrett's lack of interest. Hornby flicked the ball to Studd nearby who flashed it back to Lyttelton. Bails jumped — nine for 122. Murdoch, run out, had made an invaluable contribution of 29.

Steel's first delivery to the new batsman almost had Boyle caught. The next bowled him and so the Australians were all out for 122 — a meagre lead of 85.

Edmund Peate, unlucky the previous day, had bowled 21 overs, 9 maidens, and taken four wickets for 40.

By now it was 3.25 and one man sitting in the crowd had seen his last cricket. George Eber Spendler, aged forty-seven, of 101 Brook Street, Kennington, complained to his companion of not feeling well. He got to his feet and took only a few steps before collapsing. Blood flowed from his mouth. He was carried quickly into the nearest building — the pavilion. Here Mr Spendler was examined by several medical men, including the President of the Surrey County Cricket Club, Dr Jones. A few minutes later, Mr Spendler was pronounced dead. The diagnosis: a broken blood vessel.

The Australians, as they took to the field, were still smouldering over the Sammy Jones incident and impatient to get at Grace in particular.

By how many wickets would England win? This aspect seemed to offer the only scope for speculation among the spectators.

Frederick 'Demon' Spofforth

Hornby changed the England batting order by promoting himself to open with Grace. Barlow would come in at fall of the first wicket.

The afternoon grew chillier and the clouds darker as Murdoch set the field for Spofforth. Blackham was instructed to stand well back and this, in itself, prompted a buzz of chatter. This was hushed by Spofforth leaving his mark and gradually accelerating into full stride from the gasometer end.

Grace watched the approaching figure who seemed all arms, legs, and nose. As the Demon reached his delivery stride, WG's bat became absolutely still. The bowler's right arm whipped over and the London correspondent of *Home News*, Reginald Brooks, likened the delivery to cannon shot. It was smothered by the great bulk of Grace going forward. The master batsman then inspected the spot where the ball had pitched.

Soon Spofforth was on his way again—this delivery shorter, passing the stumps on the off side. Blackham, far back as he was, had to move very smartly. Grace continued on the defensive and a maiden over ensued.

Attention swung to Garrett at the pavilion end. He was unable to match the pace of his colleague. Hornby took a single. Grace took a single. Each batsman managed a single from Spofforth's second over.

Three more singles came—two from Garrett—before Hornby cut Garrett through the slips for the first boundary. The applause melted some of the tension. There was similar clamour when, in the same over, the England captain found 2 on the leg side. Grace saw the total to 15 by turning Garrett to square leg for 3, but England's first setback was afoot.

A rocketing full toss from Spofforth launched Hornby's bails on the breeze. Hornby had 9 to add to his couple from the first innings—sparse consolation.

Barlow came to the crease. Spofforth charged in again—and brought many to their feet as again he felled the timber. Barlow, trekking back to the pavilion, stepped over the middle stump—England two for 15.

Ulyett was next to face the fury, and he managed to avert the hat-trick.

It was the turn of Grace now to counter-attack. He drove Garrett for 3 to leg, Jones fielding a metre inside the boundary. Then Grace lofted Spofforth for 2, triggering applause and bringing the total to 20, or the target down to 65.

The crowd erupted again during Spofforth's next over as Grace, in full cry, savagely swept the paceman for 3. There was also a no-ball. Two more singles brought up 30 on the scoreboard.

As in England's first innings, Murdoch switched Spofforth to the pavilion end. There were absolutely no runs with which to be generous. Grace immediately pillaged 2 more from the lanky speedster.

Play was interrupted briefly when Boyle, who had taken over at the gasometer end, hurt a finger in trying to deny Ulyett. Grace then smashed the same bowler to the square-leg boundary. The first ball of Spofforth's next over was despatched by Ulyett in similar manner.

By now, the crowd was convinced that the two big men were running away with the match. The Demon seemed spent. The Colonials would need to dig much, much deeper for a trick to beat the old country. This conviction became more deeply etched as each batsman proceeded to find the square-leg boundary and scatter encroaching spectators. A few people, fancying more rain, even drifted homewards for tea.

After initial wavering, Boyle found the line and length to curb the batsmen. More and more frequently, Grace and Ulyett found themselves obliged to push and check, push and check. The clouds swooped low on the breeze and the light, at its best, became poor. But the rain kept off and the wicket began drying patchily—to the despair of the batsmen and the delight of the Australians. While some deliveries almost tunnelled, others decided to climb as though going up a church steeple.

The 50 crawled up at 4.35, but only a single was added to this when Ulyett edged one of the steeple climbers to Blackham. As Spofforth celebrated his third capture, Ulyett, heading back to the pavilion with 11, said to himself, 'Put the kettle on, Mother.' He called anybody 'Mother' when he wanted a cup of tea—England was three for 51.

The match, of course, was still generally considered won, and would be as long as Grace occupied a crease.

Taking up the cudgel now with Grace was the dependable right-hander, Lucas. They needed 34. Lucas found himself admiring the style with which Grace cut Boyle for 2. No effort seemed involved. Impeccable timing reaped its reward.

Boyle again. Nothing apparently special, but moving low to the off from the pitch. Grace moved with plenty of time, his bat flashing through the gloom. The ball was lofted. Without diversion, Bannerman took the catch at mid-off. Boyle knew his finest moment so far. The Australians were rid of the world's best batsman.

Four for 53—and the trickle to the gates dried up. Cigars were worked about nervously and gripped more firmly between dry lips. The bowlers now gained an aura of menace.

The fact that there was another day to obtain the runs offered no comfort to the batsmen as Spofforth and Boyle suddenly seemed a metre faster.

Lyttelton stepped into the front-line vacancy in a hush indicating that England was now considered under siege. Here, indeed, was an increasingly unhappy breed of men.

The only sound to intrude on the canopy of silence was the approaching and fading clip-clop of hansom cabs along the Vauxhall Road.

Both batsmen had early narrow escapes as each sought desperately to secure his first run. A thunderbolt from Spofforth blistered Lyttelton's trembling bails. Another equally-fiery delivery made contact and the ball

Alfred Lucas

Alfred Lyttelton

grazed Blackham's outflung glove. Somehow, Lucas survived.

Eventually Lyttelton glanced Boyle to leg. The batsmen hurtled from their creases to cross twice before the return winged in to Blackham. Minutes later, the crowd roared again as Spofforth actually erred with length. Lyttelton seized his chance. The ball flashed to the boundary.

With this, the Australians cut off all charity and began to pulse like a single entity around the tightest bowling seen that summer. The ball rarely beat the bat, yet the strikers were utterly frustrated in seeking advantage. Time froze on 65.

Some watchers started to count the maiden overs as these began to stretch out; the next would be the tenth. How much longer could the stalemate hold? Spofforth toiled in relentless silence. Boyle, with slide-rule accuracy, gave nothing.

Murdoch's friend, the drying wind, tugged at shirts and trousers. He let the screw keep turning.

Spofforth again — giving everything, giving nothing. Twelve maidens.

There was an edge and the crowd winced for the Honourable Alfred Lyttelton. A single for England.

More maidens . . . three, four . . . It was Spofforth, probing tirelessly, who found the vital gap and took the off stump. A gasp went up from the multitude. Lyttelton had made 12 — five for 66.

Half an hour of the day remained as Steel made his way to the wicket. He watched Lucas chop a slower one from Boyle through the slips for 4.

Steel took guard and prodded the first delivery from Spofforth to the off. Spofforth now came in like a runaway train and flung his everything. All Steel could do was pop it up to be caught and bowled by the Demon — six for 70.

Read was next. He middled the first ball with apparent confidence, but his middle and off stumps were horribly mauled by the next. Spofforth was mobbed by his teammates — seven for 70 and England needed 15 for victory.

The turn of Barnes now to face the onslaught and he soon smacked the Demon away for 2. Another eruption.

Then 3 byes sent the place mad — to be hushed again as suddenly by the spectral Spofforth eating the ground. From the pounded, quaking turf came up a wrecking ball. Lucas, this once a non-starter, was forced to yield an edge and played on to his stumps.

Eight for 75. England needed 10 to win. It seemed like 10 000. Studd, held back by Hornby to stop the rot, headed for the eye of the storm. First, though, he had to watch Barnes cope with Boyle. Barnes fenced with the first delivery and stroked the second back along the pitch. Boyle picked up and retraced his steps.

Near the Tavern, an umbrella handle snapped with a crack like a pistol shot, alarming those nearby and, not least, the unfortunate owner who was abruptly and cruelly denied the comfort of something to gnaw upon.

Boyle turned and steamed in. The delivery, of immaculate length, found more turn and lifted more sharply than Barnes was equal to. The ball found his glove and looped to Murdoch at close point. It looked to be the easiest catch of the day.

Murdoch, over the two days, had known rapidly alternating elation and despair, though he had betrayed nothing of this. Now he had England on their knees — needing 9.

The last man, Peate, came like a lamb into a lion's cage. Impatiently, he smote Boyle for 2. There was frenzy. The next delivery, wider to the off, he left alone.

Boyle roared in for the third delivery and the ball came off the turf like a startled red grouse. Peate countered with a sort of pelvic thrust, his bat revolving in a wild, opposing arc — and was bowled, perhaps not as cleanly as his destroyer would have wished.

In the ensuing moments of silence, the Australians began running towards the pavilion. Spofforth found himself lifted to the shoulders of his ecstatic teammates before all were engulfed in congratulatory applause.

Studd, the in-form batsman who had not faced a delivery, trudged in the wake of the Australians and reflected on his contribution. Well, he *had* caught Bannerman.

Summed up, the inquest verdict was brief and brutal: the England players had lost their nerve, in poor light on an overworked and drying pitch, against brilliant fielding and inspired bowling.

Punch put it in six lines of verse:

> Well done, Cornstalks, whipt us
>   Fair and square.
> Was it luck that tripped us?
>   Was it scare?
> Kangaroo land's 'Demon', or our own
>   Want of devil, coolness, nerve, backbone?

On the following Saturday, 2 September, the *Sporting Times* carried its mock obituary for English cricket, a mild and clean joke, but to be recalled by cricket devotees for longer than any of the other more academic observations by the pundits of the day.

The Oval Test was not, however, the end of the tour for the Australians. They were scheduled to play next against an Eleven of England at Tunbridge Wells and then against Nottinghamshire at Trent Bridge. After these encounters, they were due to visit Scarborough, Leeds, Manchester, Harrogate, and Glasgow. On 30 September, they were to sail to America for a match in New York and one in Philadelphia before travelling by rail across the United States for a game in San Francisco from where they would sail home on 21 October. Back in Australia, three matches would then be in prospect — at Adelaide in December, in Melbourne on New Year's Day, and in Sydney starting on 26 January 1883, all against a mixed — amateurs and professionals — England team, led by Ivo Bligh.

43

CHAPTER 3

How Reginald Brooks reacted to the popular reception of the mock obituary is unknown, but English cricket was quickly 'resurrected.' However, only four members of the Oval Test team—Barlow, Barnes, Steel, and Studd—were among Bligh's tourists. Of the others, Morley and W. Bates were experienced campaigners while I. F. W. Bligh himself, C. F. H. Leslie, G. F. Vernon, E. F. S. Tylecote, G. B. Studd, and W. W. Read were newcomers to the Test scene.

Ivo Francis Walter Bligh, twenty-three-years-old second son of the sixth Earl of Darnley, came from Cobham in Kent, the cradle of cricket.

About 1870, with preparation at Cheam and with the long and solid Kent tradition of cricket behind him, Bligh was sent to Eton. Here his developing athletic prowess won him a place in the school XI captained in 1876 by W. F. Forbes. That season, he made 73 against Winchester and 12 against

The England team that went in pursuit of the Ashes. From left, standing: W. Barnes, F. Morley, C. T. Studd, G. F. Vernon, C. F. H. Leslie. Seated, from left: G. B. Studd, E. F. S. Tylecote, I. F. W. Bligh (captain), A. G. Steel, W. W. Read. In front, from left: R. G. Barlow, and W. Bates

Harrow. The next year he did less well, but the lapse was temporary and, on entering Cambridge, he was awarded his Blue as a freshman. This led to his selection for the famous side captained by the Hon. Edward Lyttelton which beat, in a single-innings match in 1878, the first Australian team to take the field at Lord's.

Bligh played regularly for Cambridge from 1878 to 1881 and captained the University side in his last year there. Ivo also represented Cambridge at tennis and rackets. He seemed likely to become one of the best tennis players in the country, being able to take advantage of an enormous reach; and very strong wrists enabled him to command a heavy stroke. He played for Cambridge against Oxford in 1879 and 1880 and, in the latter year, won both the singles and doubles competitions.

Edmund Tylecote

He was equally hard-hitting in rackets and won the singles against Oxford. But it was in cricket where his future shone brightest. In 1879, his best innings was an unbeaten 113 against Surrey and that year he was at the top of the averages with Lyttelton. The next year, he made 70 and an undefeated 57 against Yorkshire, 90 against the Gentlemen, and 59 and 13 against Oxford. The same year, he scored 105 for Kent against Surrey at The Oval, and 69 not out against an England XI at Canterbury.

Bligh's vice-captain was Edmund Fernando Sutton Tylecote, a sharp wicket-keeper and sound batsman for Oxford University, Kent, and Bedfordshire. He first attracted attention by scoring an undefeated 404 at Clifton School.

William Bates was a Yorkshire round-arm, slow spinner and a sparkling batsman who had toured Australia in 1881–82; Charles Henry Frederick Leslie an all-rounder for Oxford University, Middlesex, and Shropshire;

Walter William Read a temperamental Surrey batsman with a powerful off-drive; George Brown Studd, a Cambridge University and Middlesex batsman; and George Frederick Vernon, a big hitter for Middlesex.

Among their fellow passengers for the long voyage, the cricketers found the multi-millionaire landowner and philanthropist, William Clarke, his wife, Janet, and staff, returning to Melbourne after an absence of more than a year.

While Murdoch's Australians were still playing cricket in the north of England, Bligh's twelve-strong party sailed from London on Thursday 14 September — only two weeks after the Oval Test — aboard the *Peshawur*, a mail steamer belonging to the Peninsular and Oriental Company.

The *Peshawur* was a working-class seahorse, not designed to win beauty contests. She had one funnel, two 600 h.p. engines, three masts, four decks, and a squarish stern.

The *Peshawur* arrived in Colombo, Sri Lanka (then Ceylon) on 13 October. The next day, after taking on fresh supplies, she began thumping south-east across the vastness of the Indian Ocean into sunshine and calm water. On the night of Sunday 15 October, the sky was open and starry, encouraging the ocean and the seafarers to relax.

A service on deck had finished at about nine o'clock when some of the passengers noticed a distant light, quite different to a star. As they watched it, this light drew nearer, to excite a murmur of speculation among passengers and crew throughout the vessel. Another ship was heading towards them. In the silence, the gliding approach of the stranger almost adopted the aura of a phantom.

The *Peshawur* was carrying 343 people. More and more of these sought a place on the starboard rails as Captain Edward Baker altered course to avoid risk of collision. The captain of the other vessel apparently took similar action. Inexorably, it seemed, the distance between them shrank. A passenger on the *Peshawur* describes what happened next:

'. . . Like an avalanche, there tumbled down the stairs from the quarter deck about twenty passengers and stewards. I was knocked. Somebody shouted: "A ship on top of us!"

'I rose again and scrambled out of the way. The confusion and consternation about me was awful for a few minutes. About 150 men, women, and children crowded to the aft part of the deck and eventually there was some relief.

'My wife called for her little children and you may imagine my horror as I pictured their being crushed to death, for I knew they were in bed about the spot where the ship ran into us.

'In a minute or two, I tried to descend the companion ladder into the saloon. The refreshment bar was shattered. The ice man, a native, was lying with an immense block of iron on his leg. There was a gaping hole in the ship's side . . .

'. . . On entering the saloon, I found our nurse with the youngest child in her arms. All were safe and in the cabin. Our three little boys, Jack, Reggie, and Bertie, were still sound asleep, not even wakened by the sound of the awful crash just a little above them. It was a great relief to hurry back on deck and tell my wife.

'Passengers hurriedly compared notes. Many were the miraculous escapes recorded. Where the ladies had been sitting a few minutes before, there was nothing but wreckage. An immense quantity of stones, bricks and mortar were strewn about, this being the cement from the bows of the other ship.

'Outside the refreshment bar, we also found the greater part of the bowsprit of the strange vessel, including iron work weighing nearly half a ton.

'The damage done to the *Peshawur* when she struck near our centre consisted in cutting through our waterways, splitting and twisting up the iron plating below the main deck and knocking a hole through the side four feet above the water.

'The vessel, in freeing herself, carried away the bulwarks for twenty-five feet, carried away also our gangway ladder, two large boats, that is the life-boat and the cutter, also smashing the standard compass, the door of the captain's cabin, and breaking one of the booms.

'Our first duty was to find out if our steamer was sinking as we expected, but, in a few minutes, it was reported that we were making no water and in

The *Peshawur*—Courtesy of the P & O Group

fact that we were safe. The machinery gave a few revolutions which further convinced us that all was well. The wounded native was immediately attended by two doctors and found to have his leg broken in two places.

'Next, our anxiety was for the other ship. On looking around, we found that she had not sunk for she was burning blue lights. Captain Baker gave orders to steam back close to the ship and he sent a boat in charge of the second officer, Davidson, to ascertain the extent of her injuries and to enquire if she wanted any assistance.

'The delay was somewhat painful because the boat took a considerable time in returning in consequence of our ship having to steam some distance off to avoid a second collision.

'At last, the boat drew alongside and the quartermaster shouted to Captain Baker: "Ship *Glenroy*, sir, bound from Mauritius to Madras and Calcutta. Four hundred coolies on board."

'The second officer said that the captain of the *Glenroy* had reported that the bow of his ship was completely knocked away, his fore compartment full of water, foremast badly sprung and the ship making water through her foremast watertight bulkhead, she being an old iron ship of twenty-five years' standing, her tonnage is 1,139 tons. His request that the *Peshawur* would stand by him all night was, of course, complied with . . .

'When day dawned, the full extent of the havoc was visible. We spent many hours endeavouring to make fast to the *Glenroy* in order to tow her into some port. The hawsers broke several times. Ultimately, at the suggestion of Captain Baker, two wire hawsers were made fast to the *Glenroy* cables and thirty fathoms of cable were paid out on to each hawser and, this succeeding admirably, we made sail without further trouble back to Ceylon. Only five knots per hour was the speed allowed because the other ship was making water very fast, notwithstanding all hands at work on the pumps. On Thursday morning at eight o'clock, we arrived off Galle where we signalled and obtained a pilot boat which took off our telegrams, and in the afternoon we arrived safely at Colombo without the loss of a single life.'

The spot where the accident occurred was about 580 kilometres from Colombo, and equidistant from the southern tip of Sri Lanka and the Chagos Archipelago.

An extract from the *Peshawur* log reads: 'October 15th, 1882, 9.13 pm. Collided with barque *Glenroy* which struck the ship in starboard gangway ladder, and main gaff, damaging main rigging stays and backstays.

'9.15 pm. Cleared the vessel and went on ahead. *Glenroy* head gear carried away, making water, asked to be towed into port.

'Most of the passengers on board were members of the MCC cricket team on their way to Australia to play a series of matches. Some of them had narrow escapes from falling spars . . .'

In fact, Fred Morley had damaged a rib, but he was an uncomplaining fellow, reluctant to make a fuss, and the seriousness of his injury was not realised until much later.

A court of inquiry into the collision opened in Colombo on Friday 20 October 1882. Captain Baker, of the *Peshawur*, gave the following evidence:

'I am Commander of the *Peshawur*. We were bound to King George's Sound. We left Colombo on the evening of the 14th October. The collision took place on the evening of the 15th between 10 to 15 minutes past 9. I was walking forward after reading service. When I got a little way forward—four or five paces—I saw a red light on the starboard bow about three points. I immediately rushed to the bridge, stopped the engines, put on full speed astern, and put the helm hard-a-port . . .

'The vessel was about one and a half miles off when I first saw her, as near as I could judge. The moon had gone down. It was a clear night. The wind was about WSW—a light wind. I looked over the side and aft to see if our engines were going astern, and I saw by the discharge pipe that they were. I then looked at the vessel again. I saw her sails, and saw she had starboarded her helm and was luffing right up in the wind. Her starboard bow came in sight, but there was no green light there to indicate which way she was going at the time. In a minute after this, she struck us about the after-gangway.

'I stopped the engines immediately, my ship having two to three miles way upon her at the time. We were going about 12 to 13¾ knots. Immediately after the collision took place, I went aft to the scene of the accident to ascertain what damage was done. Finding that the ship was not struck below watermark and seeing the other ship on my starboard quarter, I cleared away some of the wreckage left by the other ship, keeping the other

The *Peshawur*—Courtesy of the P & O Group

vessel in sight all the time, in case she made signals for assistance.

'I desire to add nothing more than that every assistance was rendered that could be rendered to the vessel, and we succeeded in getting her safe into port, having her in tow. I altered her course without communicating with the officer of the watch . . .'

The court adjourned for half an hour for tiffin and, on reassembly, Captain John Wright, of the *Glenroy*, gave his evidence:

'I am captain of the *Glenroy*, bound from Mauritius to Madras and Calcutta. On the evening of the 15th of October last, about fifteen minutes before 9 o'clock, I saw a bright light a little fore the port beam about two points — about six miles. It proved to be a steamer's masthead light. I was on the poop at the time. When I saw the steamer, I told the second officer to go and see if my side lights were burning brightly and he came back and reported that they were burning well. I then kept on my course, steering north-east. As I saw the steamer approach, and as it did not seem to keep away, I went forward myself and saw my own side lights — red and the green light on the starboard side — burning. When I did that I was about three miles off and the steamer was approaching me rapidly.

'When she came a little closer, I shouted to them: "Why don't you keep your ship away?" Someone answered from the steamboat: "Keep your own ship away." When the steamer said "Keep away," I was still keeping my course. I then considered that if I kept my course, the steamer would run me down. I called to the man at the wheel to put the helm hard a starboard. Then the ship came up to the wind, and collided. As soon as the ship collided, the starboard light was smashed to pieces. I took the steamer to be going full speed all the time. I thought that if I did not luff, she would run me down.

'The wind was WNW on the port side. The collision took place about eight to ten minutes past nine o'clock. I don't remember hearing the two bells strike on my own ship before the collision, nor did I hear it from the other ship. I did not see the steamer's side lights till about five minutes before the collision. My side lights can be seen on a clear night (from) at least three miles. It was a clear night. When I luffed the steamer, she was a little on the port bow — not far off. We just cleared the steamer's bows as we came round.'

Richard Barlow, in evidence, said: 'I am a passenger on the SS *Peshawur* to Adelaide. I remember the night of the collision. The collision took place about ten minutes past nine. I was standing by the saloon door, looking over the ship's side. I saw something in sight — a dark object and no light. A minute or two later, I turned round to see if any of our cricketers were about, to tell them about this something in sight. I turned round again and saw a red light at sea out in the direction where I had seen the dark object and the time I saw the red light, it might be two or three minutes. I only saw the red light. I watched the ship until it struck us — it took a curve and ran round right into us. I saw no other light.'

50

W. W. Read, in evidence, said: 'I am a passenger in the *Peshawur* bound for Australia. I remember the collision on the 15th. I was almost amidships. I was looking across the sea. I turned my head away for a few seconds and when I looked again, I saw a large red light where I had seen the dark object before. It struck me at once as being a very brilliant light. I saw no other light. I saw the other vessel until it came up within a short distance. I always saw the red light after I first saw it. I saw the vessel within a few yards until it struck.'

Walter Read

The judgement of the court was that the *Glenroy* never had any green light during the night, and only put up her red light a few minutes before the collision.

The evidence of the *Glenroy*'s doctor and officers was disbelieved. The nautical assessor mathematically proved by diagrams that the *Glenroy* could not have been in the position described by her officers, while the *Peshawur*'s position was directly rendered according to what happened at the time of the collision.

Captain Wright's certificate was suspended for six months. Captain Baker was exonerated. The question of damages was left to the Vice-Admiralty Court.

While in Colombo, the passengers on the *Peshawur* wrote to Captain Baker:

'Dear Sir: We, the undersigned first-class passengers of the *Peshawur*, on our voyage from London to Australia, are anxious to express, before separating,

51

our gratitude to you for your courteous and obliging conduct, and our perfect confidence in you as a sailor. We have watched the extreme care you have taken of our lives in foggy weather, and in parts difficult of navigation; and your unflinching and self-denying devotion to your duty has won our fullest respect. We wish to assure you of our deep sympathy with you in the present trying circumstances; we need scarcely say that our recent accident has, in no wise, shaken our trust in you.

'So far from that, it is our hope that arrangements may be made for you to take us to our destination in your good ship. To you, as the responsible person, our thanks are first of all due; but we beg you to express to your officers and crew on our behalf, our high appreciation of the energy, skill and courage which they have shown throughout the voyage, and especially at the crisis when these were most called for.

'We are, dear sir, yours faithfully.

'W. J. Clarke, Joshua J. Farr, J. Henniker Heaton, James J. Fitzgerald, Charles J. Prescott, Jas. Scott, Wm. Henry Harrison, N. G. Elder, Fred. C. Boyer, Herbert H. Christophers, J. Alfred Jeffreys, Chas. Moore, David Tweedie, Edwd. L. Yencken, Edward Jones Pitman, Lewis Conran, Allan G. Steel, E. F. S. Tylecote, W. Barnes, C. E. Butler, Joseph Bryant, L. Coope Smith, Charles F. Studd, Ivo Bligh, R. G. Barlow, H. E. Medlicott, A. Cooper, H. E. Williams.

'Lily Snodgrass, Blanche Clarke, Janet Clarke, Jane Farr, Walter Wm. Read, Isabella Grieve, John Howe, Jane Bakewell, Ellen Tweedie, Lydia Warren, G. Ross, Margaret Ross, Sophie C. Fenton, Ethel M. Clarke, Walter Lucas, Annie T. Prescott, Alice Rostron, Edith J. Alford, May Alford, Maude Lyons, L. C. Kerrich (Lieut 4th Light Cavalry), A. S. Judge, John Kaines, Elizabeth W. Kaines, R. P. Moore, Chas. Edward James, Jessie Elder, Annie L. Elder, M. L. Fitzgerald, J. N. Elder, Laura J. Crisp, S. B. Spiro, W. Bates, M. V. Burnett, Maggie Fitzgerald, F. Morley, George B. Studd, Rose Heaton, John Holme, Mr & Mrs Banberger, C. F. H. Leslie, May Hobson, M. R. Cobbett, George F. Vernon.'

Captain Baker replied: 'Ladies and Gentlemen — Allow me on behalf of myself, officers and crew, to express our sincere thanks for the kindly feelings you entertain towards us. I can only assure you that all have done their best to make your voyage happy and comfortable.

'Equally with yourselves, I regret the collision which has somewhat marred a pleasant voyage. I cannot help feeling grieved at it, but allow me to assure you that my grief has been much lessened by the kind sympathetic expressions you have just given utterance to. Wishing you a pleasant continuance of your voyage . . .'

CHAPTER 4

Fred Morley's rib, subsequently found to be broken, was not the only worry for the cricketers at the start of the tour. Ivo Bligh badly injured his right hand, not in the collision, but during a tug-of-war on the ship. He was consequently unable to take part in the first six matches. The first of these was played in Adelaide on Friday and Saturday, 10 and 11 November, against Fifteen of South Australia.

Tylecote won the toss and elected to bat. The weather was dull and cold with frequent showers. About 1000 spectators saw England lose six wickets for 45. Barnes and Tylecote hoisted the century, however, Tylecote making 59 and Barnes 42. They were all out for 153.

Frederick Morley

On the second day, the South Australians had made 128 for seven when the match was abandoned as a draw. Morley had managed to bowl 19 overs, 12 maidens, and capture three wickets for 17.

While in Adelaide, Bligh made a speech in which he referred jokingly to the Ashes. This at first mystified the Australians who had not recently been to England. As soon as the joke was explained to them, however, they appreciated it and considered young Ivo, with his arm in a sling, a fair dinkum aristocrat.

The tourists moved on to Melbourne and were soon guests at a dinner party given at Rupertswood, the country home in Sunbury of William Clarke who had been on the *Peshawur*.

The Clarkes' original wealth was accumulated during a lifetime of astonishing dedication by William John Turner Clarke (1805–74) who became a living legend.

Born with a deformed hip which was always an aggravating burden, he nevertheless developed the stature of a John Wayne with a West Country voice probably like that of the former cricket commentator, John Arlott. This was 'Big' Clarke.

Orphaned and penniless in Bridgewater, Somerset, at the age of thirteen, he was, however, fortunate to be among the younger of eight children and therefore had a lot of relatives and friends. His early dexterity in mental arithmetic was some compensation for his physical deformity.

William went to work on the farm of his uncle, Joseph, for only board and lodging. But Joseph had two sons of his own and soon William had to look elsewhere for work. So, at fifteen, by virtue of his skilled horsemanship, he became a drover's boy — walking from Taunton in Somerset to the Smithfield Market in London. Soon he was earning up to $4 a week — several times the amount earned by a farm labourer then.

At school, William had been acquainted with the maxim: 'A penny saved is a penny earned.' With this he coupled: 'Look after the pence and the pounds will look after themselves.' It became the philosophy which served him too well ever to desert.

While his peers spent as they earned, William saved furiously and, at twenty-one, was an independent livestock dealer.

When he was twenty-four, he eloped with a clergyman's daughter, Eliza Dowling, and they immediately emigrated to Tasmania (then Van Diemen's Land) with a few shrewdly selected cattle and horses and some Leicester sheep.

After a hazardous voyage during which they were chased by pirates, they reached Hobart on 23 December 1829. William immediately hired fields for his stock, then sought from the Government the maximum land grant which had motivated his emigration with capital of £1500. The maximum grant was 1037 hectares but William, with his strictly limited means, in the official view, was allowed only 810 hectares.

This, however, was the vital foothold he needed, and he devoted virtually the rest of his life to acquiring more property and raising sheep.

Tasmania was soon too small for him. He crossed to the mainland and bought extensive properties in Victoria, South Australia, and finally New Zealand. His setbacks were insignificant against his acquisitions. He was twice elected to the Victorian Legislative Assembly and, when he died at the age of sixty-eight, early in 1874, he left a fortune today worth between $120 million and $160 million.

'Big' Clarke left all his Victorian properties to his eldest son, William, who spent lavishly and soon began building the Rupertswood mansion.

The English cricketers' second match was in Melbourne against Eleven of Victoria. This started on Friday, 17 November. Again, Tylecote won the toss and decided to bat on a fine day and faultless wicket before about 6000 spectators. They saw some fine batting from Bates, C. T. Studd, and Leslie. The England innings ended with Morley being bowled by W. Bruce for 3. The total was 273 with Leslie not out 51.

At this stage Morley became too ill to take further part, but Read and Steel were soon taking wickets and, with a total of 104, Victoria were forced to follow on. This time, the home side made a better start, but even so were all out for 169. Thus England were obliged to bat again — for one run. The first delivery went for 4 byes, giving the tourists victory by ten wickets.

On the second day of this match, Murdoch and his team arrived home in the SS *City of New York* to an enthusiastic welcome. They were given a banquet in Sydney and another reception on reaching Melbourne.

Meanwhile, the England party went on to play against Twenty-two of Sandhurst, Twenty-two of Castlemaine, a New South Wales XI, Eighteen of Maitland, Eighteen of Newcastle, and Eighteen of Ballarat, finishing there on Thursday 28 December. Bligh and his men then returned to Melbourne for the first of the battles to 'recover' the Ashes.

CHAPTER 5

Bligh, who had recovered sufficiently to play at Newcastle and Ballarat, was fully fit for the first Test match. This started in Melbourne on Saturday 30 December 1882. Morley, however, was still not well enough to play. His place was taken by Vernon.

McDonnell and Palmer, who had missed the Oval Test, were back in the Australian side to the exclusion of Boyle and Jones. Percy Stanislaus McDonnell (Victoria, New South Wales, and Queensland) was an attacking right-hand batsman with a solid defence. He was remembered for scoring 147 in the third Test in Sydney in 1881–82. George Eugene Palmer (Victoria and Tasmania) was a right-arm, medium-fast spin bowler and good on any type of wicket. During the first Test at the Oval in 1880, he took three of the five wickets to fall in England's second innings.

The 1773 George III penny used by Bligh to toss in the Tests in Australia

A good batting wicket now awaited the side lucky enough to win the toss. It was Murdoch's lucky day. The umpires were J. Swift and E. H. Elliott.

The action began with Charlie Studd bowling from the railway end to Bannerman with Bligh at point, Vernon long-on, Barlow third man, Read mid-on, Steel forward cover, Bates mid-off, George Studd extra mid-off, Barnes at slip, and Leslie long-off with Tylecote at the stumps. The batsman chanced nothing and Studd recorded his first maiden over.

Attention quickly focused on the contrasting styles of the batsmen. Bannerman firm in the belief that if he stayed there runs would come; Massie intent on making as many runs as quickly as he could while the going was good.

Barnes, from the pavilion end, took up the issue with Massie whose urgency was immediately obvious. The last delivery of the four-ball over from the medium-pace Nottinghamshire man streaked to the square-leg boundary.

Studd again to Bannerman who drove to mid-off and took a single. At first, this looked comfortable enough, but a splendid return from Bates had Bannerman stretching to make his ground. Bannerman retained the bowling and Barnes achieved his first maiden. One run from two overs was not Massie's idea of cricket. He advanced on Studd, driving hard, straight—and up. Charlie Studd flung himself. Australia one for 5, of which Massie had made 4.

Murdoch dealt studiously with the two remaining balls of the over. The Barnes/Bannerman dual resumed and the little opener won applause by chopping for 3. Murdoch chanced nothing and another Bannerman–Studd exchange went down as a maiden. Ten came up when Murdoch turned Barnes to leg for 2. Charlie Studd might have taken his second wicket when Bannerman put him uppishly through the slips. Barnes missed it—2 runs.

Striving to make amends, Barnes tested Murdoch's defence with good line and length—a maiden; and a maiden from Studd. Barnes paid the penalty for straying as Murdoch cut him for 3. These were the last runs for a while. Seven successive maidens were punctuated now and then by applause for bowling and fielding exploits. The run drought was broken when Bannerman cut Barnes for 4. But three more maidens went down before Bannerman managed to push Barnes to the off for a single. In this fashion, the total climbed to 20.

At 24, the first bowling change was made. Barnes was rested for Steel's right-arm slow spinners, but these did nothing to change the tempo. A single was flicked here, another there. Thirty crept up and brought more bowling changes—Barlow for Studd and Read, with under-arms, for Steel. At lunch, Australia was one for 46 with Murdoch on 23 and Bannerman 19.

The break encouraged Murdoch to come out of his shell and the scoring rate suddenly accelerated with a flourish of boundaries. Sixty was reached and Bligh tried to stem the flow by bringing back Studd.

With the total at 70, the round-arm Bates took over from Read. Eighty came up and Bligh now pulled a surprise by bringing on the Oxford captain, Leslie, not often considered as a bowler. He took a long run and flung down rather wildly. Murdoch weighed this up for a couple of overs, decided there was little there but pace and stepped out swinging. Leslie took the off stump and his first Test wicket. Australia two for 81. Murdoch had fallen two short of his half-century. Bannerman awaited his third partner.

Horan was playing at home and the crowd expected much from him but he got a top edge to Leslie and Barlow, at slip, took a fine catch. Australia three for 81 —and Leslie on a hat-trick. McDonnell, however, denied him that glory

57

and went immediately into a display of fine strokes, all along the ground except for a moment when he lofted dangerously close over the head of Charlie Studd.

The dismissal of Bannerman surprised everybody—except perhaps Bligh who expected the stumps to fall with each delivery. Going forward to Leslie, Bannerman's back foot cleared the ground momentarily. He happened to be beaten for once by the pace. Tylecote whipped the bails off, his appeal rising to a scream of delight. Australia four for 96. The anchor man had gone for 30.

Giffen launched himself with a boundary and the strokes continued. Anything loose was punished. When it became obvious that Leslie was no longer a deterrent, Bligh brought back Steel who learned the hard way not to send down the occasional lob for variety. With 150 hoisted, McDonnell flayed Bates straight to Read. The ball was too hot for him to hold. Twelve runs later, Bates reaped the wicket earlier denied him. He clean bowled McDonnell for 43. Australia five for 162.

Next to the crease was Bonnor. Bligh immediately tried to tempt him with Leslie, but the big hitter reined in. Against Steel, however, he gave way to his natural inclination. Once he was almost run out in being sent back after nearly reaching Giffen's stumps.

Twice the ball cleared the picket fence near the pavilion, reaping 10 in all but in trying to emulate his partner, Giffen was stumped by Tylecote off Steel for 36. Australia six for 190.

Blackham joined Bonnor who continued to swing with devastating force. Another towering shot, off Bates, went into the elm trees for 5. Reaching 30, Bonnor gave another chance from Steel's bowling, but yet again Read was unable to hang on. Instead of a wicket falling, 4 more runs accrued to bring up 200.

Blackham's innings was a mixture of good luck and good management. Moments occurred when he seemed bemused by his own achievement. With 220 on the board, Read took over from Steel and the field spread even wider. Bonnor gave good reason for this by hitting his fourth 5.

The fielders watched helplessly and the scoreboard soon showed 240. Bonnor cut Barlow uppishly but safely for 3, taking his score to 51. With the landmark of 250 reached, perhaps Blackham, on 25, momentarily relaxed his vigilance. An edge off Charlie Studd again delighted Tylecote—Australia seven for 251 in fading light.

Spofforth came to the crease. The Demon had registered a single and Bonnor had cruised on to 60 by stumps. Australia would go into the second day and the New Year with 258 for seven. In the meantime, there were celebrations for everybody. The England team headed for Rupertswood where, in addition to the New Year, they helped to celebrate William Clarke's elevation to a baronetcy—the first Australian to be honoured in this manner.

Heavy rain came with the New Year. On a damp Monday wicket, the batsmen scored their early runs with caution, the ground drying all the while. After 270 had been reached, deliveries began rising nastily. Spofforth, failing to keep these down, was missed first by Barlow and then by Tylecote. Bonnor, predictably, recorded the first two boundaries of the day with straight drives off Barlow.

The first to fall was Spofforth, on 9, who mistimed in heaving at Barnes. Steel, in the long field, manoeuvred under the ball—Australia eight for 289.

Garrett's tenancy was brief. In attempting to drive Steel for his first run, he lofted to Charlie Studd—Australia nine for 289.

George Bonnor

The last man was Palmer. Bonnor needed 15 for his century when his hopes were dashed as he edged Barlow to Barnes at slip. Australia, all out for 291, would now, it seemed, be aided and abetted by a turncoat wicket.

Viewing their prospects none too happily, Barlow and Bligh opened for England. Barlow faced Spofforth with Blackham at the stumps, Bonnor at slip, Horan short leg, Giffen long-on, Massie mid-off, Garrett forward cover, Murdoch point, Palmer mid-on, Bannerman mid-off, and McDonnell third man. The first over was a maiden. The field changed for Palmer to take up the attack, Bligh shaping to receive him. Another maiden. Bligh was clearly troubled by the lift and turn outside the off stump.

Barlow picked Spofforth off his legs for 2; and did nothing more before Palmer splayed Bligh's stumps. The England captain departed, still needing his first Test-match run.

On a similar quest, Leslie came to the crease. Apprehensively, he watched Barlow deal with more sizzlers from the Demon. For all his expression betrayed, the Lancashire professional might have been alone in the middle of a paddock enjoying the serenity.

Could Leslie survive until lunch? Twice he worked Palmer away for 2, there was a bye, then a shorter ball gathered extra venom in pitching, took a top edge and went into Garrett's hands at forward cover — England two for seven at lunch.

Charlie Studd emerged with Barlow to start the second session. Spofforth's first delivery beat him. So did the second. The third sent Studd's stumps flying. It was his third successive Test innings without scoring — England three for eight.

Steel came to try to haul England out of the mire. The Melbourne wicket now bristled with all the villainy that had been exhibited by The Oval towards the England side on that black August day only a few months ago. Now, as then, singles prompted applause normally accorded to boundaries. The first truly aggressive shot for an age was struck by Barlow. The batsmen raced back and forth to add 4. Twenty came up, and 30 without further loss. Steel late cut to the boundary and at last it began to seem that Spofforth might be reduced to mortal dimensions.

But the fire that seemed to die in Spofforth flared in Palmer. Barlow, in going forward, lost the line. Blackham whirled. Momentarily the bails lived. The partnership of the Lancastrians became history. Barlow had made 10 — England four for 36.

With Read now at the other end, Steel decided to take the Demon by his horns and cut successive deliveries to the boundary. The 20 000 crowd, sympathetic to the Englishmen by this time, responded warmly.

Palmer was having none of it. Swinging to the off, the ball turned to flash through a gap momentarily between bat and pad. Steel, his stumps shattered, headed for the pavilion — England five for 45 and utterly bewildered.

Bates came to do his best. Would it be good enough? For a while, he poked and jabbed. He did lots of gardening. At the other end, Read's strokes became more assured. He middled the ball regularly. After he turned Spofforth to leg for 3, the scoreboard showed 50.

Three maidens were bowled and then Bates turned Spofforth to leg for a couple. Garrett replaced Spofforth, but 60 came up without further loss, and 70. The sun appeared and began to sooth the wicket. The total crawled to 80, then leapt as Bates stepped back daintily and cut Garrett to the grandstand. Soon after this, he was dropped by Spofforth and then by McDonnell. The Yorkshireman lunged into his third life by hitting Garrett out of the ground for 5.

With England moving through the 90s, the Australians adopted a keener approach — and Read, in trying to glance Palmer, was bowled round his legs. The visitors, at six for 96, were still far from the bright uplands, despite the sun.

Tylecote saw the 100 up with Bates and this hard-won achievement was marked by a sharp shower. The players sprinted for the pavilion, but were obliged to stay for only a few minutes. On the restart, Bates drove the first delivery from Garrett straight into Bannerman's hands at mid-off.

England seven for 100. With the sun shining and before another delivery could be sent down, the rain returned. When the players came out again, George Studd accompanied Tylecote.

With the total on 117, a misunderstanding between the batsmen found them both at one end. Blackham, who had left his position to collect a wild return, raced to destroy the stumps at the opposite end. George Studd abandoned his attempt to get home. England had eight wickets down.

William Barnes

Barnes came to Tylecote's support and the Nottinghamshire professional became the anchor man. Tylecote showed his strokes to bring up 130. He continued busily and before long was taking applause for bringing up 150. Immediately after this, Blackham failed in a dazzling attempt to stump the pacemaker. A few deliveries later, Tylecote lived dangerously again when he edged through the slips fractionally wide of Bonnor's awesome leap. In the same over, and before Tylecote could score again, Palmer bowled him for 33 — England nine for 156.

That brought together Vernon and Barnes. Vernon, another making his Test debut, began scoring with apparent ease from both Spofforth and Palmer. He had made a confident 11 when the middle stump at the other end was uprooted. Barnes had made 26. Palmer had taken seven for 65 in a spell unbroken from the start. The Englishmen, with a total of 177, were invited to follow on.

Ominously, Barlow found himself opening for England twice in the day. This time, Tylecote was with him, Bligh having dropped himself down the batting order. The immediately objective was merely to survive until stumps. In achieving this, they made 11.

More showers during the night did nothing to improve the wicket. At noon on the Tuesday, however, the weather was fine though dull, and the match resumed.

Barlow and Tylecote quickly established an entertaining scoring rate against Spofforth and Palmer. Thirty soon came up. In the 30s, however, Tylecote was twice beaten when Spofforth turned very fast balls from the off. Each time, the Oxford amateur survived stumping appeals from his Australian counterpart. Fifty came up in little more than half an hour. Murdoch made his first bowling change by introducing Giffen's slow-medium brand. Immediately the South Australian presented Barlow with problems. And at the other end, Spofforth was quickly improving on his line and length.

Sixty was approached much more slowly. At 64, Spofforth pitched one wide of the off stump, deceived Tylecote with the turn and stole the off bail. The England wicketkeeper departed, having made 38.

Charlie Studd came out for his fourth Test innings, still seeking his first Test run—and was immediately in trouble again coping with the remainder of the Demon's over. He survived, however, and next found himself facing Giffen's tantalisers after Barlow had glanced a single. It was with relief, therefore, that he turned a ball to leg for 2. Barlow continued his struggle against Spofforth and another maiden was recorded. Studd shaped up to Giffen again and was able to drive a ball tossed higher than the usual through the covers for his first boundary. A cut forward of point gave him 2 more. Barlow fenced through another mean maiden from Spofforth. Giffen again. Studd took a single to mid-on. He played another maiden from Spofforth, still far from happy against the fast man.

Palmer returned to the fray and Barlow, glad of the extra pace, took a single from his second delivery. This put the Lancastrian back in Spofforth's sights—and the Demon bowled him off his pads for 28—England two for 75.

Studd, not out with 9, was joined by Steel who took off with three rapid singles. Each batsman then took a single off Spofforth. Steel's fourth run brought up 80. Palmer bowled a maiden, the tightest imaginable, and might also have claimed a wicket as Studd conceded an edge to the slips. In that moment, however, Giffen got a fly in his eye and the chance went begging. Impatient with his colleague, Spofforth kicked the ball and the batsman darted through for a single from the resulting overthrow.

Studd glanced Palmer for a single. Spofforth chalked up an angry maiden. Palmer was also glanced by Steel and this delicate touch yielded a boundary. It also took the England total to 86 for the loss of two wickets as the sides went in for lunch.

Although Spofforth began the afternoon session with another maiden to

Studd, the Cambridge man was beginning to get the measure of the Demon. Runs came steadily, though without much drama, and it was Studd who brought the total to 100 with 3 to leg at the expense of Spofforth. In the same over, Steel flashed to the square-leg boundary.

For the first time in the match, the prospect was beginning to look brighter for England but then Palmer struck again. Studd moved to cover one outside the off stump, was totally beaten by the turn and blanched at his collapsed furniture. He had made 21.

England, three for 105, still lagged behind the Australians' first innings total by 9. With a lot to be done yet to save the match, the England captain was cheered to the wicket. Bligh saw out Palmer's over, pushing the last ball to mid-off for a single. The luckless skipper managed two more singles before losing his stumps to one of the Demon's special snorters.

England four for 108 and again threatened by collapse. It became Read's task to help check the Demon. Six runs were still needed to level matters. Read concentrated on settling in, while Steel looked for any runs that might be in the offing.

An Australian second innings soon became necessary as the immediate crisis passed and the new partnership began to flourish. Runs were made on both sides of the wicket from both ends — until Murdoch brought back Giffen with his slow-medium spinners. Steel, soon tempted to pull, was beaten by the flight and trapped lbw for 29 — one better than in his first innings — England five for 132, a lead of 18.

Leslie, who was not well, became Read's partner and their understanding brought up the 150. Palmer bowled a maiden and applause for this had hardly died when Giffen produced an innocuous delivery which, nevertheless, skittled Leslie who was on four — England six for 150 and in deep trouble.

Bates proved slow but steady. After two singles, he drove to the long-on boundary. The partnership had put on 14 when Read, with a polished 29, went rather rashly down the wicket to a short-pitched ball from Giffen. Read made contact, but the ball still succeeded in eluding him to break the stumps — England seven for 164.

George Studd did his defensive best in support of Bates. Facing a new over from Giffen, he went forward defensively as usual with the desired consequence. Giffen picked up, returned to his mark, then offered a teasing floater that just begged for a sweeping. Utterly convinced of doing precisely that, Studd swept — to give Palmer the sweetest of catches at mid-on — England eight for 164, 49 ahead.

Barnes made his entrance. Bates now tried to hit Palmer over the pavilion. His ambition was thwarted, however, by Massie who raced in from long-off to take a fine catch by the conclusion of which he had slithered to a sitting position — England nine for 164.

Vernon appeared and cracked Giffen for 3 to leg. Barnes cut the same bowler for 2. Palmer engaged Vernon and was soon asking the question. He was duly credited with the second lbw of the innings — England all out for

169. Murdoch's men needed 56 to win. With a rapidly-improving wicket, there could be little real doubt now about the outcome.

When Massie was caught and bowled, for the second time in the match, by Barnes, without an Australian run on the board, the England players could have been tempted to have fleeting visions of a reversal of The Oval nightmare. However, Bannerman and Murdoch, as they settled in, soon demolished the basis for any such creeping fantasy. Carefully, and with increasing confidence, the pair steered their side to a comfortable victory. Bannerman hit the boundary that won the match and took him to 25. At the other end, Murdoch had 33.

Hugh Massie

CHAPTER 6

Successive defeats of England by the Australians, first at The Oval in London and now in Melbourne, was simply too much for *The Times* of London to stomach. Accordingly, it reversed the outcome of the second encounter:

'Melbourne, Jan. 2: The first match between the Australian Eleven and the Hon. Ivo Bligh's team commenced yesterday, and concluded today. The Englishmen won by nine wickets. Morley was absent.' For good measure this 'victory' was achieved, according to *The Times*, in two days—thus matching the Australians' feat at The Oval. Touche!

In preparation for the second Test, also to be staged in Melbourne, Ivo Bligh and his men went to Tasmania. At Launceston, on 8 and 9 January, they played against Eighteen of Northern Tasmania. Neither Leslie nor Morley were able to take part in this match. The special correspondent of the *Sportsman*, Mr M. Cobbett, was recruited by the tourists. The home side batted first and made 144. For the visitors, Charlie Studd, opening with his captain, contributed 99 to a total of 270. Bligh, with 34, was the second highest scorer. Cobbett batted last and was bowled by Oldmeadow for nought. The Tasmanians, in their second innings, could raise only 86. Steel, with a helpful wind, took ten for 33. England won by an innings and 75 runs.

The Englishmen went next to Hobart and there encountered Eighteen of Southern Tasmania. The home side won the toss and batted first on a difficult wicket for a total of 82. Bligh, opening again, was the top scorer for England with 32. Only Steel (21), Barnes (15), and George Studd (13) were able to stay long with their captain. The side made 110—gaining a lead of 28. At second bidding, Southern Tasmania made 95 and England won by seven wickets.

With these peculiar victories behind them, the tourists went back to Melbourne for the crunch match—the Test they must win for the sake of Queen and country; and to keep alive the spark among the Ashes . . .

Friday 19 January 1883, was fine with a light southerly breeze. The Melbourne Cricket Ground wicket was dry and fast.

From the England dressing-room came the news that Fred Morley was fit to play and Vernon was consequently omitted from the side. The Australian side was unchanged—to the chagrin of the locals who believed that Boyle ought to have been chosen. Swift and Elliott were again the umpires.

Bligh won the toss and had no hesitation in batting first. This time it was Charlie Studd who opened with Barlow. Spofforth, as usual, opened the bowling, aided by Palmer.

For Spofforth, Massie was at mid-off, Bonnor long-on, Horan square-leg,

Giffen short-leg, Murdoch point, Bannerman short mid-off, Garrett cover, McDonnell slip, and Palmer forward cover.

Barlow, at the railway end, took first strike. Each bowler began with a maiden and the first run came when Barlow worked Spofforth past point. Surprisingly, the first 11 runs came from Barlow. Eventually, Studd opened up by driving Spofforth through the covers for 4. Barlow then had some difficulty with Palmer who bowled another maiden. Studd cut Spofforth for 2, 2 more with greater force, and a single—all pleasing to the eye. Barlow safely lofted Spofforth for 2 to bring up 20.

Allan Steel

Studd next attacked Palmer, hitting him to square leg for 3. Facing Spofforth again, he drove straight and had settled happily for 2—until Palmer misfielded and allowed a boundary.

Palmer at last found some turn from the off. Studd, on 14, lost the line and his middle stump—England one for 28.

Leslie arrived at the wicket and, before he had taken strike, saw Barlow put Spofforth among the cluster of fielders on the off—but the ball went to the ground.

A willing workhorse, Palmer toiled on steadily and when the total was 35 he beat Barlow with a fine delivery that achieved some movement in the air to take the Lancastrian's leg stump. Barlow had also made 14—two for 35. Palmer took credit for both wickets.

Leslie's new partner was Steel. This pair settled in and saw 50 up.

66

Murdoch then rested Spofforth in favour of Giffen at the pavilion end. However, the batsmen continued to indulge in some fine strokes. Leslie, in sweeping to leg, brought a superb right-handed stop from Horan. The Irishman's return not only denied a run, but made Leslie stretch desperately for the crease. At lunch, the total was 68 without further loss.

On the resumption, Leslie soon swung high and safely to long-on. Not everything was to the batsmen's liking, though. Palmer, continually striving for variety, made one turn and lift nastily to force Steel's hasty retreat. Leslie, at times seeming half-hearted and listless, made a few eyes blink when the ball rebounded from the grandstand pickets.

Ninety, but there was a fright for the Englishmen before the century as Palmer almost caught Steel from his own bowling. Touching the ball, he diverted it and Bannerman nearby narrowly failed to complete the dismissal.

Two off Spofforth brought up the century and made Leslie's 50, but only 6 were added after this before Australia claimed the next wicket. Leslie, on 54, went for an apparently safe single. Spofforth, square with the bowler's wicket, had one stump at which to aim: he felled it with the Oxford man well short of the crease—England three for 106.

The new man was Read, as cautious as a pavilion mouse with half a tail. The scoring rate slumped. At 130, Blackham missed a stumping opportunity in expecting the ball to take Read's off stump without his intervention. Giffen came on for Palmer. A slow, slow teaser and Steel, on 39, went to drive—unwisely. At mid-on, McDonnell took a very comfortable catch—four for 131.

Read was developing fine form by now. Barnes joined him and quickly settled in. There was generous applause for the 150. Spofforth and Palmer came back, but the scoring rate, if anything, increased. At 170, Barnes was keen for a single and set off, but Read stayed at home. Barnes became stranded and a run-out seemed a certainty. In moving backwards to take the return, however, Spofforth fell over the stumps. Barnes lived to battle on.

When 180 was hoisted, Giffen returned for Palmer. Soon the change of pace brought its reward as a Giffen delivery did just enough to nudge the bails. Barnes had contributed an extremely valuable 32—England was five for 193.

No matter which end he found himself at, Tylecote, on this occasion, looked extremely unhappy. Twice he stumbled in getting to the pitch of Giffen and twice he groped outside the off-stump for Spofforth. He watched Read add 6 more runs, including a boundary off Spofforth. Then Giffen again was doing things in the air and, eventually to Tylecote's leg stump—England six for 199.

The England captain was applauded to the crease. He watched Garrett bowl a maiden to Read before facing Giffen who was bolstered by his triumphs. Bligh pushed the first straight back down the wicket and did the same with the next. The third he intended pushing to the off, but it went out on the leg side. The last, going down the leg side, nipped back late and bowled him—England seven for 199, after being four for 193.

Another maiden from Spofforth to Read. Bates was now at the opposite end and without more ado, the swarthy Yorkshireman swung high towards the long-on boundary where Horan was unable to manoeuvre properly and consequently missed a hard chance. The resulting single brought applause for the 200.

Bates seemed determined to knock the South Australian out of the attack. Successive boundaries flashed through the covers and another drive in the same direction yielded 2.

At 216, Blackham missed a chance of stumping Read who was on 42. Both batsmen continued hitting freely to hoist 230. At 234, Palmer came back, but to no avail and at stumps on the first day, England was seven for 248.

During the night the weather turned sultry and there were some showers. On resumption, Read and Bates continued in their grand fashion. Both gave some difficult chances, but were still together at 280.

At 286, Palmer changed ends and Garrett took the ball at the other. This change of tactics worked. Bates, advancing and driving Palmer, was this time taken by Horan at long-off for 55—England eight for 287.

Read, joined by George Studd, added 6 more before Palmer caught the Surrey man from his own bowling. The amateur's polished 75 had provided the necessary backbone to the innings.

England were nine for 293 as Morley was cheered to the wicket. Studd pushed a single then became Palmer's fifth victim, bowled, with the total at 294. The medium-pace man had bowled 66·3 overs, 25 of them maidens, and conceded 103 runs.

The wicket was rolled and 50 minutes before lunch, Bannerman and Massie began chasing the England total. In the event, Bannerman left the actual chasing to Massie. The last three England wickets had put on 46 runs in fifty minutes. Massie, to judge from the first over he received from Charlie Studd, seemed bent on bettering this rate.

Studd, of medium pace, came in from the railway end and Massie pushed forward with deceptive care to a good-length delivery. The second was shorter, going to leg with obliging lift. Massie swept: his first 4. Studd again, on target, but slightly overpitched. Massie forward, driving straight: his second boundary. The last ball of the over was wide of the leg stump. Massie, on the move, was very tempted, but somehow managed to contain himself. Tylecote sprawled in vain: 2 byes—Australia 10 without loss.

Fred Morley had an unusually small head and lacked the obvious physical strength generally associated with a fast bowler. His strength was in his length and direction. He came in from the pavilion end to take issue with Bannerman. The stonewaller was in no mood to emulate his partner. The very idea of scoring a run from the first over in a Test match might even have been offensive to him. The virtually obligatory maiden ensued.

There was a general stir of expectancy again as Studd galloped towards

How a cartoonist saw Australia's batsmen during the second Test at Melbourne in 1883

the stumps. Massie fidgeted. The delivery, however, offered him no safe scope. The ball rolled out on the off to be met by George Studd who picked up and flicked back to his brother. Massie's patience ran out during Studd's next run in. He stepped back to cut. There was clinical precision: his third 4. Studd again. Massie hooked — 4 more. The Sydney man's next extravagance was a straight drive, but Read's smart collection and return permitted only a single — Australia 19 without loss after three overs.

What would happen now? For the first time, the tear-away Massie faced England's fast man. And the flood of runs was stemmed — temporarily, anyhow. The over produced a leg bye.

The Massie-Studd battle again: a cut for 2 was followed by an intended drive that took an outside edge and went wide of slip for 3. Retaining the strike, Massie went down on one knee in sweeping the Nottinghamshire bowler to the boundary to renewed applause.

A maiden from Studd to Bannerman came as an almost welcome respite. Barnes was now introduced as an attacking force. Massie went on blithely cutting and driving, but could no longer find gaps as frequently.

For the last over of the session, Morley was given the railway end. To Bannerman, the idea of a run at this stage would also have been offensive and Morley thus recorded his second maiden. Massie, with his 26, went to lunch thinking of what he might have scored. Bannerman, still to contribute, cared not a fig . . .

Ivo Bligh did not appear for the afternoon session. He had lumbago and George Alexander substituted for him. Alexander, a Victorian, had played in the Oval Test of 1880 and was now the England team's tour manager. He had substituted for Morley in the matches at Sandhurst and Newcastle.

In trying to find his rhythm again at the pavilion end, Morley sent down a rare loose ball and at last Alec Bannerman felt able to push a single. The volume of the applause for this was more usually associated with a boundary.

Barnes bowled a maiden from the railway end. Massie advertised his intentions by cutting Morley to the scoreboard, but then found himself pinned down.

With 40 on the board, Morley bowled a maiden to Bannerman. Massie flicked Barnes away to leg for 2. There was another maiden from Morley. Massie took a single to short leg. In taking the second of two leg byes, Massie was almost run out.

After being hit by Massie for 4 to long-on, Barnes was replaced by Barlow. Massie hit the new bowler's first delivery to mid-off for a single. Bannerman brought the total to 50 by cutting Barlow through the legs of Steel who was suffering from severe dysentery.

Morley made one lift sharply. Massie, in trouble for the first time, played uppishly to mid-on, but there was no chance of a catch. Some maidens, some singles; and Massie, in lashing at a ball well up from Barlow, was cleanly bowled — Australia was one for 56, a satisfying start.

Supported by his captain now, Bannerman steered through two more maidens. Then he turned Morley for a single and cut Barlow quite savagely forward of point for 3. Sixty came — and stuck there through eight consecutive maidens. Credit for these went mainly to George Studd for some incredible fielding at close mid-off. During this run drought, Bates relieved Morley and Murdoch cut Barlow to point where Steel dropped a difficult chance. Relieved only by 4 byes, the maidens continued, stretching out to fourteen. It was Bannerman who put an end to the stalemate. He took a stride down the wicket and swept Bates to leg for 4. Encouraged by this audacity, Murdoch, after half an hour and a life at the crease, stole through for his first run when Morley fumbled at mid-on.

Murdoch soon took another single, this time to leg, at Barlow's expense. Yet another single came to the Australian skipper, this one from Bates. Seventy was reached when Bannerman cut the Yorkshire spinner for 2.

Two more maidens and Barnes relieved Barlow as a sharp shower flitted across the ground. Events about to unfold caused many reflections on that shower.

In his next over, Bates bowled Bannerman. Had the few drops of rain enabled the spinner to get an extra degree of turn? — Australia two for 72.

It was Horan's turn now to share the crease. The second delivery from Bates he turned behind square leg for 3 and consequently faced the next over from Barnes. The third delivery of this was overpitched. Horan drove hard but upwards. The bowler, stretching his big, lean frame to its limit, took a superb catch above his head — Australia three for 75.

Next in was the student of Greek, McDonnell. He immediately cut Barnes for 3 to retain the strike. The first delivery he faced from Bates took his middle and off stump — Australia four for 78. That shower probably had done something.

Giffen came out frowning around at the light that was not bad, but had only recently been much better. He lofted the first offering from Bates gently back to the mildly surprised bowler — Australia five for 78. There must have been something in that shower. Many put blind faith in Bonnor.

What happened next was described later by Allan Steel in the *Badminton Book of Cricket*:

'Somebody suggested that, in the faint hope of securing a "hat" for Bates, we should bring a silly mid-on. Bates faithfully promised to bowl a fast shortish ball between the leg and the wicket, and said he was quite certain that Bonnor would play slowly forward to it. Acting on the faith of this, W. W. Read boldly volunteered to stand silly mid-on. In came the giant—loud were the shouts of welcome from the larrikins' throats . . . as Bates began to walk to the wicket to bowl, nearer and nearer crept our brave mid-on; a slow forward stroke to a fast shortish leg stump ball landed the ball in his hands not more than six feet from the bat. The crowd could not believe it and Bonnor was simply thunderstruck at mid-on's impertinence; but Bates had done the hat-trick for all that, and what is more, he got a very smart silver hat for his pains . . .'

William Bates

This feat by Bates was not the first Test hat-trick. Yes, of course, it was the Demon who had already taken the credit for that: at Melbourne on 2 January 1879, Spofforth's six for 48 during England's first innings included the dismissal with successive deliveries of the Reverend Vernon Peter Fanshawe Archer Royle, of Oxford University and Lancashire; Francis Alexander MacKinnon (The 35th MacKinnon of MacKinnon) of Cambridge University and Kent; and Thomas Emmett who captained Yorkshire from 1878 to 1882.

Billy Bates did not become the first man in Test cricket to take four wickets with successive deliveries. Blackham denied him this feat by turning the wily spinner to leg for a single. But that shower certainly had done something.

71

The wicket-keeper stayed with Murdoch long enough to begin reviving hopes for Australia. Barnes bowled a maiden and each batsman pushed a single to have 80 hoisted. Blackham then drove Bates for a single, turned a shorter one from Barnes for 2. He made allowance for the next ball to turn, but it carried straight through, taking the leg stump.

Australia, at seven for 85, now had to rely on bowlers to support the captain who seemed to have been starved of the strike. Garrett joined him and the scoring rate picked up again. Garrett soon had a single and Murdoch took the total to 90 by sweeping Bates to the square-leg boundary. Another to Murdoch left Garrett to cope with Bates. The number eight batsman stepped out and drove hard on the volley to long-off. There was only a single in it until an erratic return from Leslie, who was also a victim of dysentery, went for 4 overthrows. The excitement triggered a clamour around the ground. Garrett, his confidence growing, soon hammered Bates for 3 more. This stroke brought an ovation for the century.

With the total at 104, however, Garrett went to the pitch of Bates once too often, missed, and turned to see his stumps looking rather silly. He had made 10.

Eight wickets down. Murdoch, a lonely figure isolated from the jubilation, awaited Palmer's support. Palmer, like Spofforth, preferred to bowl.

Murdoch drove Barnes for a single. Two maidens then ensued. Palmer eventually despatched Barnes to leg for a boundary and next a single to bring up 110. Palmer turned Barnes neatly to leg for 2. Barlow replaced Barnes. Murdoch got a faint touch to the last of Barlow's first over, but Tylecote failed to hold a difficult chance.

Palmer, on 7, survived a nasty delivery from Bates, only to mistime the next, a yorker, and be bowled—Australia nine for 114.

Barlow bowled a maiden to Murdoch and so it became the turn of Spofforth to face the baffling Bates. The Demon stroked the first back along the wicket. The second turned in sharply from outside the off stump and bowled him.

Only Murdoch, unbeaten with 19 made in two and a half hours, had been able to cope with Bates. The Yorkshireman had bowled 26·2 overs, fourteen maidens, and taken seven for 28. His first victim had been Bannerman immediately after that shower. With a total of 114 it was the Australians this time who were obliged to follow on . . .

At 5.30, Murdoch and Bannerman began chasing 180 to avoid an innings defeat, but their more immediate aim was that both should survive until stumps at six.

Predictably, Bates, from the railway end, opened the bowling to Alec Bannerman and, even more predictably, the Yorkshireman recorded his fifteenth maiden of the day.

From the pavilion end, Bates continued the attack. Murdoch got an edge through the slips, uncomfortably near Bates, for 3. In the next over from Bates, Murdoch took a single to leg. Barlow induced another poor stroke

72

from the Australian skipper and the ball went fractionally wide of Tylecote for another charmed 3.

Facing Bates again, Murdoch picked the ball off his toes and the batsmen ran 4. These took Australia into double figures. The next ball was cut for 2. A misfield by Barnes gave Bannerman his first 2 runs at Barlow's expense. In the same over, he glanced to leg for 2 more.

Again Murdoch took Bates beautifully from his toes. Four more, all run, and 21 went on the board. Barlow and Bannerman duelled through another maiden, then Bates' teasing was rewarded when he lifted Murdoch's bails— Australia was one for 21, of which Murdoch had made 17.

Blackham was the night watchman and the new partnership saw out the remaining minutes. At stumps, the total was 28 with Bannerman on 5 and Blackham 6.

The weather was cloudy but bright and fine for the resumption of play on the Monday. The Englishmen found these conditions more comfortable than the harsh Australian sunlight which could make judging catches difficult. Bligh, recovered by now from his attack of lumbago, led his side on to the field. Bates, from his now beloved railway end, started the day with a maiden to Bannerman. Barlow did even better. He scattered Blackham's stumps with his first delivery. Australia two for 28.

Bonnor came to the crease far earlier than he had hoped would be necessary. He took a single to square leg and then prepared for a battle of wits with Bates. The Australian Hercules was still bristling from the manner of his dismissal in the first innings. His eyes swept the field—no silly mid-on this time—and finally settled on the waiting Bates.

Bonnor stretched gigantically forward for bat to rendezvous safely with the ball in what was by now regarded by the Australian batsmen as an infamous patch of turf outside the right-handers' off stump at the pavilion end. The next delivery was straighter but fractionally overpitched. Feet, arms, and bat flowed in perfect harmony. Bonnor did not even think about running. Neither did the fielders. Four along the ground behind square-leg. The next was despatched in the same direction, but safely high and over the heads of the front-row spectators for 5.

The crowd had been waiting for this. The hubbub continued while Bannerman patted and stroked at a few deliveries, then died out completely as attention returned to Barlow trundling in. The action swung along to Bonnor who tested the covers with a fluent drive for 3. The ball looped its way back to Barlow who brought a gasp from thousands of throats as he forced an edge from Bannerman only to see the golden chance missed by Bates in the slips. The opener still needed to improve on his Saturday tally of 5.

Bates to Bonnor and necks craned. Five more—out of the ground . . . Barlow to Bonnor—only a single, but 50 on the scoreboard. Bates to Bonnor again, and another towering 5 vanished from sight. Bligh decided that was enough and rested poor Bates in favour of pace. Could Morley stop the flood? The fast man massaged his rib cage as he measured out his run. His second delivery Bonnor tucked away for a single, the third Bannerman cut for 3, and the fourth Bonnor lashed for 3. Morley's expression said: 'What can you do?' Bligh had a grin, a few words, and a pat on the shoulder for him. Barlow again — to be driven with relish by the giant to the chains. As suddenly as it erupted, however, Bonnor's blaze was extinguished. Intent on more punishment for Barlow, he mistimed in sweeping and was caught, appropriately by Morley at mid-on for 34.

Tom Horan

Australia three for 66. The field was brought in very tight to greet Horan who fended away the remaining delivery from Barlow. Of course, Bates returned immediately. Bannerman swept the first, a loosish effort, behind square-leg to the boundary. These runs brought the total to 70. The second delivery was also overpitched and Bannerman cracked it into the covers wide of Bligh who, nevertheless, succeeded in preventing more than 2. The third went in the same direction but through the air and Bligh, a cruising tower of strength, had no problem in taking the catch. Bannerman, undone by an extraordinarily uncharacteristic flourish, had made 14 and Australia was four for 72.

Disappointing the crowd with only 3 runs each in the first innings, Horan and his new partner, McDonnell, became intent on establishing themselves. For Australia, it was essential that they should stay there.

McDonnell eventually forced Barlow to long-off for 3, then Horan tried to do similarly with Bates. The ball bobbed. Steel flung himself. His fingertips made contact — that was all.

Fine strokes came from both bats. Eighty and, after some dawdling, 90. At 93, Horan, on 15, struck low and hard to deep mid-on. It was not the sort of catch Morley would be expected to miss—and, indeed, he held it safely. Australia's fifth wicket was down and Bates had his tenth victim of the match.

There was a general alert with the entrance of Massie. Immediately he clubbed the bamboozling Bates to square-leg for 3. A boundary was prevented only by intervention of Leslie's foot. McDonnell worked a single and the next delivery from Bates was bludgeoned by Massie, this time comfortably beating Leslie to the square-leg boundary. That stroke brought the century, but Australia still needed 80 to make England bat again. So much now depended on Massie. Would he rise to the occasion? The powerful right-hander from New South Wales busied himself by driving into the covers. There was only a single as Bligh loped for it. Massie collected 2 more in turning Barlow to square leg.

Bligh toyed with the idea of bringing back Morley—no, he would give Massie a little more rope. Bates continued. Massie lashed out at three consecutive deliveries. He missed the first two. The third sailed high towards the long-on boundary. Nobody was out there and it looked as though he would get away with it. However, Charlie Studd, with the sort of burst that could be attributed nowadays to a four-minute-mile aspirant, finally launched himself for a catch that jerked spectators to their feet in appreciation as the player kicked his heels triumphantly towards the sky. Australia six for 104 and staggering.

Joined by Giffen, McDonnell continued calmly with some fine, clean strokes. Attacking, he drove Barlow to the long-on boundary and Bates along the same tracks for 2. The scoreboard ran up 110. Giffen, who had been the second of Bates's hat-trick victims, avoided any repetition by gliding Barlow through the slips to the fence, and also driving Bates to the boundary. McDonnell took a dainty single off Barlow to retain the strike against Bates. McDonnell, on 13, was looking quietly confident by now, but again Bates pitched into the devil's little acre as the batsman went through the motion of pushing gently forward. The off stump looked for a drunk to lean on. Australia seven for 113.

The next man to the wicket was Garrett. He was happy to let Giffen take the reins. The South Australian ripped into Barlow for 3 to long-off and pounded Bates to the square-leg boundary. Up went 120.

Garrett managed a well-run single from Barlow and Bates floated down yet another maiden. Barlow almost caught Giffen off his own bowling. The drive was straight and hard. Barlow took the sting out of it. A single was scuttled. Time for lunch . . .

When he drove the last delivery of the first over of the afternoon, Giffen denied Bates another maiden and enhanced his own tally by 3. Giffen continued with a cover shot for a single from Barlow.

Garrett got a top edge that made him blink. Tylecote waltzed momentarily but the ball broke away and Garrett began a second life.

With a beautiful sweeping of Bates to square leg, Giffen brought up 130. The batsmen ran four as Morley had some difficulty throwing in. Playing Barlow to short-leg, Garrett collected a couple, but Giffen only made his ground to loud appeals and jumping bails. This narrow shave was short-lived, however, as Bates again conjured some enigmatic response from outside the off stump to get that extra twist and turn. Helplessly Giffen watched the ball carry to Bligh at point. He had made an entertaining 19 and Australia was eight for 132.

Resuming with Palmer now at the other end, Garrett put Barlow to short-leg for a single, and lifted Bates over mid-off for 2.

Palmer handsomely carved Barlow to the square-leg boundary, but Garrett, goaded by Bates, hit out, and lifted to long-on, there to test the eye of Barnes who did not allow the jeers of some spectators close behind to distract him. Garrett had contributed 10 to the total of 139. Bates had thirteen wickets. Could he equal his first innings' feat?

Spofforth came out for the last stand and immediately displayed the fire more readily associated with his bowling. For as long as he was able, he would get on with the job. He made a good start by driving Barlow straight to the pickets, then for 2 into the covers. Palmer fenced through another over from Bates without event. Barlow to Spofforth again. Applause erupted as the ball bounced back from the pavilion fence; and again for almost a replay. Inside five minutes, Spofforth had made 14, putting to shame some who had preceded him.

But now Palmer had to cope with Bates—and the inevitable. He tried to hit Bates out of the contest as Bonnor had succeeded in doing. Unfortunately, he lacked the weaponry. He came from his crease fighting and found the middle well enough. The fault was in the angle of contact. The ball scorched high and free. Alas, it did not get beyond the reach of George Brown Studd who performed athletically at deep mid-off.

Ivo Bligh's men, despite their aches and pains, had fought back to win by an innings and 27 runs. In the pavilion, champagne and speeches flowed and Billy Bates was the toast of the town. A collection raised £31 for him and he also received a silver hat. He had bowled, in all, twenty-seven maidens and taken seven for 28 and seven for 74. The total haul, however, had cost him 12 more runs than the total conceded by Spofforth for his fourteen wickets at The Oval. Spofforth had taken 14 for 90, Bates 14 for 102.

CHAPTER 7

After practice sessions in Sydney on Thursday 25 January, the eve of the third Test, the Australian captain, William Murdoch, objected to the Lancashire professional, Richard Barlow, wearing metal spikes on his boots during the match. The Australian leader claimed that these would tear the wicket.

The professionals in the England team—Barlow, Barnes, Bates, and Morley—pointed out that Murdoch had not protested about the spikes until his team was beaten. At Ivo Bligh's request, however, Barlow removed the spikes.

On the public holiday to celebrate the anniversary of the founding of their colony, New South Welshmen, in 1883, were offered three major attractions—a sailing regatta on the Parramatta River, horse-racing at Randwick, and international cricket at Moore Park. More than 20 000 of them were drawn to Moore Park where the England captain, Ivo Bligh, won the toss. A warm sun tempered by a fresh sea breeze helped him decide to bat. The couch-grass oval promised a lot of runs. The captains agreed on the use of two wickets, each side occupying one of these exclusively.

The teams were unchanged and the first batsmen up were Barlow and Charlie Studd. Giffen opened the bowling with slow-medium pace. For this, Murdoch put himself at point as usual, Bonnor at long-on, Massie forward cover, Horan square-leg, Garrett third man, Spofforth slip, McDonnell short-leg, Bannerman close mid-off, and Palmer at deeper mid-off. Barlow took first strike.

The action began sedately with a maiden, and there was also a maiden from Palmer to Studd. Barlow made the first runs with a straight drive through the legs of Giffen. In the same over, Barlow secured 2 more, this time straight again, but wide of Giffen's legs and groping hand. Studd picked off a single, then delicately glanced to leg for the first boundary. Barlow, confident of another boundary in driving Palmer, stayed in his ground, but Massie, covering the ground with the swiftness of a hunted stag, cut off the ball before it could reach the fence. In his urgency to return the ball, however, it slipped from his fingers. Only at this stage did the batsmen decide to scamper for a single. Spontaneous applause had quickly died, but then it revved again weakly.

A total of 10 showed on the scoreboard, then 20. At 26, Spofforth relieved Giffen and immediately bowled a maiden to Studd, the final delivery outside the off-stump and really smacking into Blackham's gloves. At 38, Garrett came on for Palmer and Barlow flicked his third ball to leg for 2.

The first chance, difficult, was from Studd off Spofforth. Murdoch, at point, made a futile snatch at the red blur low to his left. One run later, however, Studd fell to a fine catch at the wicket by Blackham off Garrett—England one for 41.

Leslie came to the vacant end and two maiden overs ensued. Spofforth seemed to be increasing his pace with each delivery. The breeze was helping him, too. There were gasps as Leslie hung out his bat perilously, twice failing to make contact. Blackham had his work cut out to prevent byes. Barlow forced the less fearsome Garrett into the covers for 2 and glanced a single. Facing Spofforth again, Leslie was deceived by one initially wide of the off-stump. He was bowled without offering a stroke. England was two for 44.

Steel came in. He took a run immediately by putting Spofforth to short-leg. Barlow turned the Demon for 2 on the same side. Bannerman dived when Steel cut Garrett, but the resulting 3 brought the total to 50. Steel, keeping the strike, timed Spofforth nicely for a single to point. Perfect timing brought the Cambridge and Lancashire man 4 when he cut Spofforth square to the fence. A much later cut went for a single and gave Barlow the opportunity to do what he could about the Demon. Without ado, he thundered the speedster to the long-on boundary. With 61 on the board, Murdoch brought back Palmer to try some more slow-medium treatment. Steel immediately sliced 2 and pulled to the square-leg boundary.

Spofforth took the ball again for the last over before lunch. Perhaps Barlow, with his flawless 28, let thoughts of the lunch menu momentarily distract him. Spofforth gave the ball fractionally more liberty and Barlow went for the cover drive that fraction of a second late. The catch at point was hard even for Murdoch. Rolling, he hung on to the very acceptable aperitif.

England was three for 67 at lunch and a new batsman would face the afternoon. Steel was still there, looking solid with 17. As the players disappeared into the pavilion, the Artillery Band struck up.

Every vantage point in the ground was occupied as Read came out with Steel for the next session. Murdoch persevered with his pace attack. A bye was the first addition to the total, and then Read drove Garrett to the on for a single. Spoffforth let fly with a bumper and Steel put it up evasively to short-leg. Horan dived enthusiastically, but in vain. Read nudged Garrett to leg for another single. Garrett's last ball of that over was a yorker. Steel whirled, and, without having added to his tally of the morning, heard his stumps shatter—England was four for 69.

With Barnes at the wicket, Read took from successive Spofforth deliveries first 2 and then a single. Barnes began his own contribution in spritely manner by glancing Garrett to leg for 2. Barnes had done well during practice the previous day and it was thought that he might well be a formidable obstacle to the Australians. The wicket by now, however, was not reacting as well as expected. Several times Spofforth, as he pounded away, sent turf flying. Barnes went up on his toes to get on top of another sizzler, but it went through him and Blackham, arms flung high, was urgently asking the question. Barnes stood his ground—until he saw the umpire's finger.

England, with five for 75, had suddenly become in need of a solid stand. Tylecote, coming out, would do all he knew to help bring this about.

Behind the stumps, Blackham was bobbing about in kangaroo fashion, but he misread one from Garrett, expecting it to bowl Read. That close! Read continued, unperturbed. Tylecote gradually settled in, despite failing light as the sun slunk behind curling clouds and from Port Jackson Bay came a rumbling of thunder.

Some fine pace bowling was met with impressive strokes. Read was always eager to get on to his front foot and punished to the off whenever he succeeded in this. Tylecote was more free with strokes all round the wicket and comfortable in either stepping back or advancing. The century was greeted with a clamour. Soon Murdoch had tried all his recognised bowlers, and anything vaguely to the off was hammered into the covers. Tylecote was the least tidy of the batting pair and once he lofted forward of point. This was certainly a chance, but Garrett and Murdoch each left it to the other. The total surged to 120, then fell away again with the approach of darker clouds. These hurried on westward, however, and it became brighter again. Giffen relieved Spofforth and Tylecote welcomed the slower man by hitting his first over spiritedly for 9. In the run race, Tylecote kept well ahead of his partner. They doubled the total since joining forces and pressed on.

At 185, Murdoch resorted to Bannerman and the academic McDonnell. The break came sooner than Murdoch could have hoped—in McDonnell's first over, though the bowler was denied the credit. Tylecote, on 66, pushed to short-leg and went for a single when Horan seemed to stumble. The fielder quickly recovered to send in a superb return. Blackham flashed the bails off with Tylecote still having a couple of metres to make.

With England six for 191, the partnership for the sixth wicket had produced 116 to put a fresh complexion on the match.

Read's new partner was Bates, fresh from his Melbourne triumph. The run rate accelerated again, Bates getting under way with a couple to leg off McDonnell. In Bannerman's next over, Read turned him to leg for 2 and there was a bye. The 200 came up with Read driving McDonnell all along the turf for 4. Bates began to swing all around the wicket. An edge flew through the slips, but offered no chance. Bannerman was blazed to the boundary, and next McDonnell. After Bates was almost run out, the batsmen sobered and Bannerman actually bowled a maiden to Read. Murdoch put an end to McDonnell's suffering and brought back Spofforth.

Bates immediately late cut the Demon for a single and Read turned him to leg for 2, thus bringing his own tally to 66—equalling Tylecote's score. Bates picked off a string of singles. Eventually, Murdoch's persistence with Bannerman paid off when Read hoisted him to long-on where Massie only needed to take a few sidling steps for the catch.

England was seven for 223 and appreciation of Read's splendid knock was expressed in the applause.

With George Studd guarding the opposite end, Bates soon drove Bannerman for a single and actually advanced, swinging, on Spofforth. He middled the ball well enough, but it went high rather than far. McDonnell collected comfortably at long-on.

England eight for 224 and there was a general cheer as Bligh, tall and straight as a flagpole, made his appearance. More singles, two to each batsman. Spofforth bowled a maiden to Bligh, then Palmer took the ball in place of Bannerman. But cutting Palmer somewhat ungainly for 3, the England captain brought up 230.

In the next over, Bligh demonstrated his front-foot preference by lashing Spofforth to long-on for 2. Facing Spofforth again, Bligh stepped across with growing authority and cut the Demon for 3 more. Some byes and the total became 240. More singles were pushed and glanced. Bligh stretched for Palmer. The ball swung briskly off the seam to clip the off stump and Bligh departed, having made 13.

George Giffen

Nine for 244 and as Bligh strode off, a few heavy drops of rain prompted some stroking of cheeks and frowning at wet fingers. Fred Morley was one of the cheek brushers as he hastened towards the stumps.

George Studd pushed Spofforth to mid-on for a single. Spofforth again and the left-handed Nottinghamshire man swung through with unexpected assurance. The ball ripped back past Spofforth to long-off for 2 with acclaim.

Engaging Studd, Palmer again conspired with the wicket to beat the bat and weed out the middle and off stumps and England was thus dismissed

80

for 247. Studd had made 3 and Morley was unbeaten on 2. The players trooped off and the rain, never more than half-hearted, fizzled out.

For Australia's innings, the stumps were moved to a fresh wicket. Twenty minutes of play remained when Bannerman, this time accompanied by Giffen, emerged to occupy the crease. Bates was first to bowl. Giffen pushed him to leg for a single. He did the same in Morley's first over. Four maidens were then bowled. Giffen ended this sequence by driving Bates for 2 to mid-on. Morley was no-balled and Steel took over from Bates. Three more maidens went before Giffen glanced Morley to leg for a single. Bannerman decided that was a good example and emulated it. Australia was 8 without loss at stumps and the Anniversary Day crowd went home well satisfied.

There was rain during the night, and showers on the Saturday morning until 10.30. By noon, it was fine, though cool and cloudy, with a distinct threat of more rain. Moore Park had been thoroughly soaked.

England's opening bowlers were Barlow and Morley. Not until the fourth over was a run ventured. Giffen took this liberty with Morley, and then another with Barlow. Bannerman, as usual, bided his time, occasionally bestowing a sardonic smile on offerings outside the off stump. He watched Giffen pull Morley square for 2 and for a single; watched also Giffen drop the bat as the South Australian was struck painfully on the knee by one from Barlow.

After the pause for Giffen's recovery, Bannerman spotted the delivery for which he had been waiting. Morley was still in his follow-through as the ball romped to the boundary behind point. Bannerman went gardening. The next one was short and moved away slightly. The Sydney man clipped late and sweetly — 2 through the slips. The growing crowd expressed its pleasure with the local lad. Two byes brought up 20. The wicket was easier than expected. Barlow allowed too much air and Giffen despatched the ball to long-on. The nearest fielder was still changing direction when the ball hit the fence.

Bligh persisted with Barlow who could occasionally make one lift. Morley gave way to Bates, a guarantee of regular maidens. Bannerman, becoming more and more at home in every sense, twice stroked Barlow to the boundary. Barnes was introduced. Bannerman welcomed him with another 4 to bring up the 50 and the crowd was delighted. Four more strokes took Australia into the 60s. Bates retired for Charlie Studd who bowled a maiden to Bannerman. In Studd's second over, Bannerman glanced for 2 and an on-drive brought him 2 more. A maiden from Barnes to Giffen was the last over before lunch. Australia was 72 without loss. Giffen was on 40 and Bannerman 28.

Heavy rain prolonged the lunch interval by twenty minutes, but the army band kept everybody cheerful. When Barlow began the afternoon session, Bannerman swung his second delivery for 3 into the covers. Giffen blasted in the same direction, lacked the timing, but was dropped by Bates. The Yorkshireman's spirits were soon restored, however, when he bamboozled

Giffen and Tylecote successfully lifted the bails. Australia was one for 76 and the light was fading.

Four maidens were bowled before Murdoch, the newcomer, tapped Bates for a single. Bannerman was again deep in a waiting game. It was Bates who eventually obliged with a tempter down the leg side, but Bannerman eliminated all risk in collecting his sixth boundary—80 up. Murdoch's second run came from Barlow. This gave Bannerman opportunity for his next boundary. Bates conceded Murdoch's third run which was the prelude to three maidens. Bannerman pulled Bates with awesome power. Morley at mid-on fumbled. Somebody in the crowd shouted: 'Catches win matches!' Morley could have done without the reminder. Murdoch drove Bates for 2— and then straight into the hands of Leslie at long-off, but the Oxford captain juggled wretchedly—90 up. Bannerman swept Barlow to square leg for 2, and for 4. Bates yielded 2 to Murdoch and 2 more to put the century on the board.

The heavens opened. It was 3.30. Several inspections of the wicket later, at 5.15, play was resumed.

The next boundary was for Bannerman off Barlow and made the total 110. Charlie Studd came back for Bates and promptly bowled three maidens. Bannerman coloured some singles and byes by grandly driving Barlow to the long-on fence. This stroke made him the top scorer, an accomplishment fully appreciated by the crowd. Bannerman had another life when he edged Steel to slip. Barnes dived, but too late and all the Nottinghamshire man could clutch at was frustration. More maidens—four of them. Bannerman struck a single from Steel, Murdoch a 2, and a single as the batsmen hung on for stumps. Charlie Studd wound up the day with another maiden, leaving Australia to sleep at one for 133. Bannerman, with 68, had carried his bat through the day and Murdoch was still there with 17.

Rain developed again that night, and continued through Sunday. At dawn on the Monday, the ground was a dancing quagmire, but later the downpour began to ease, then faded out, giving way to hot sunshine. Similar weather in Melbourne would have prevented any play for two or three days, but the Moore Park turf dried very quickly, attributed to its sandy composition.

Due to some misunderstanding, play was resumed earlier than most people were expecting. The telegraph officials were among those caught napping. A wicket had fallen before they managed to reach the ground and there was impatience among those who were waiting to flash the news to Melbourne.

In drying so quickly, terrible things had happened to the wicket and it was now a batsman's nightmare or a bowler's paradise, depending on the view. The first delivery, from Steel to Bannerman, was inadvertently skied to square-leg for 3. Bannerman next took an easy single to long-on from Bates. The Yorkshireman then conjured something really nasty. Murdoch had time only to swat. He lost the ball, but dashed down the wicket at Bannerman's urging.

That first wicket to fall was Murdoch's. Steel swung in with a low shooter and before the Australian captain could clamp down he was rapped on the pads — to be the first lbw victim. Australia was two for 140.

As he departed with 19, Murdoch realised that the wicket was likely to go from bad to worse and, accordingly, shuffled the batting order to give his big hitters an early opportunity.

McDonnell was next to the wicket. The newcomer managed to push out Steel's first delivery, but the second yorked him — three for 140.

Horan took up the struggle and now there was a rare spectacle: Bannerman setting the pace, doing most of the scoring. Three boundaries were garnished with singles and pairs. The crowd buzzed as Barlow and Bates took the punishment. Horan brought the total to 150 with a single off Bates. A few minutes later, Horan was thrashing again at Bates. Morley fielded smartly at mid-on and Bannerman ought to have been easily run out, but Bates bungled the return, whipping the bails off with his hands.

Bannerman, with yet another life, stroked freely even to the off. With a couple from Bates, he brought up 170. Horan saw in good time a full toss from Morley and flashed through the covers without intervention. Barnes bowled a maiden. Morley bowled a maiden. Steel came back for Barnes and each batsman pushed a single. Then Bannerman, in trying to sweep Morley, got a top edge and Bates this time made no mistake at third man. Bannerman had made a most peculiar 94. There was a standing ovation for his departure but Australia was four for 176.

The return of Steel paid off handsomely when he had the new batsman, Massie, caught at point by Bligh for nought — five for 176.

Could big Bonnor, with Horan, hold Australia together? Horan scored 2 more before Bonnor cracked Morley into the covers. On current performance by the England fielders, this was not a chance — but George Studd, running under the ball and away with it, took an astonishing catch as the ball dropped in over his shoulder.

Australia was six for 178 — and the England side jubilant. Bonnor headed back to the pavilion with a nought in successive Tests.

What would Blackham do? A hush came over the ground. After pushing Steel for a single, Blackham narrowly escaped being run out in completing a couple for Horan. Speculation bubbled everywhere. After a maiden from each bowler, Blackham drove Morley virtually straight, the ball missing Horan's stumps — and Horan a third of the way down the wicket — by a whisker. With 194 on the board, Blackham put Steel just wide of Bligh for 2. Morley forced an edge from Horan who was on 19. Steel flung himself to collect very low and left-handed — seven down for 196.

Morley was getting more and more lift as the wicket took a baking. Garrett fenced with him — and gave an edge which was snapped up by Barlow in the slips. Eight wickets gone and the total was still 196.

Palmer took guard and immediately found himself embattled. Neither end offered respite. The 200 was hoisted when Blackham managed to take

Morley off his toes. A succession of singles and 2s brought the tally to 211. At this point, Barlow replaced Steel and tied down Blackham for a maiden.

Runs continued to be forced from Morley, but Barlow bowled two more maidens. Morley gave way to Barnes who caught Palmer in two minds with his second delivery, the ball popping up to mid-off where George Studd found his second catch of the innings a much easier proposition. Palmer had made 7 and Australia was nine for 218. Spofforth's entrance was delayed for lunch. Blackham, on 27, had earned a breather.

The afternoon began with a maiden from Barnes to Spofforth. The Demon was deprived of further opportunity as Barlow skittled Blackham with the total still on 218. The turf by this time was looking more like a ploughed field than a cricket oval.

Tom Garrett

For England, Morley had taken four for 47 and Steel three for 27. The tourists had a first innings' lead of 29.

Two Charlies, Studd and Leslie, began England's second innings. The wicket had been mown and rolled. They examined with great suspicion. Seeking to consolidate the slender lead, Studd faced Spofforth. The first three deliveries fizzed outside the off stump. The last was shorter. Steel chopped for 2.

Garrett began with a maiden to Leslie and during Spofforth's next over, Studd, too, was glad merely to survive. Leslie's first runs came when he cut Garrett backward of point to the boundary. The Demon then forced Studd on to his toes with a steeple climber. The next delivery had Blackham appealing for a catch behind, but umpire Swift was not interested. Leslie glanced Garrett for 3 to fine leg. Studd found a single and 10 came on the board. Leslie retained the bowling with another single, but lost the line of a Spofforth snorter which just touched the off stump. England was one for 13.

It was easy for supporters of the old country to fancy that Spofforth, in his impatience, pawed the ground as he waited for Barlow to take guard. The Lancashire professional was unflinching, however, and drove the paceman straight and hard — but not hard enough to beat Palmer moving across from mid-off. Another thundering off-drive. Palmer again. Applause. Garrett erratically to Studd: 4, 2, and 1 brought up 20.

Spofforth, obviously finding his element, pounded down three successive maidens, each delivery rising to at least chest height. Blackham, sweating heavily, did a good job, reluctantly but gradually putting more distance between himself and the stumps with Spofforth's increasing ferocity.

Garrett again and Barlow found his first run by pushing into the covers. Studd began a second life after Garrett missed a cruel chance off his own bowling.

Spofforth came in short and rearing down the leg side. Barlow hooked to the fence. Studd swept Garrett a few degrees less than perfectly and the dawdling ball was snatched up virtually on the boundary. The batsman crossed for 3. With the total at 29, Garrett was rested for Palmer. The Victorian medium-pace spinner was immediately despatched to the boundary; in his next over for 2, and in his third to the boundary again. Palmer and Spofforth swapped ends and Palmer was immediately driven straight by Barlow for 4.

Spofforth, thriving on his new view, brought one back very late and sharp. Studd jabbed. Stumps careered. England was two for 45 and remembering better times.

Steel joined Barlow and immediately put Spofforth through the slips for a couple. Palmer again and Barlow carved him magnificently to the boundary forward of square-leg. England into the 50s, but on 55 Steel, with 6 to his name, was trapped lbw by Spofforth. Three wickets down.

Read took his place at the crease and many spectators reflected on his polished contribution of 66 to the first innings. He saw away safely the last ball of Spofforth's over. Palmer, having found again his line and length, bowled a maiden to Barlow. Read joined the runmakers when, in Spofforth's next over, he forced 2 and a single. Palmer conceded no runs in his next over, but there were 2 leg byes and 4 byes. Timing well, Read smashed Palmer for his first boundary. His second boundary was at the Demon's expense. The next ball, fired in very short, had Blackham leaping and clawing in vain. Four byes. Palmer gave nothing. Spofforth's turn once more and Read, roaring along, crashed another boundary.

Garrett came back for a short burst. He gave way to Horan's variation on medium pace. Horan's very first delivery scattered Read's stumps. The Surrey amateur had made a rumbustious 21. England was four for 87 and not amused.

A test of patience on the threshold of the nerve-wracking 90s began with the entrance of the valued Nottinghamshire all-rounder, Barnes. A run drought ended with Barnes driving Spofforth for a single. Four more maidens. Barlow drove Spofforth for 3. Barnes pulled the Demon behind square leg for 2.

At 94, Barlow put up Horan to Palmer at silly mid-off. He had made a studious 24. England, with five down, were teetering. Tylecote would try to restore some equilibrium. Before he was able to score, however, Barnes fell to Spofforth — the Demon's second lbw victim — England six for 94.

Bates came and slammed Spofforth over mid-on but only for a single, and edged Horan through the slips for 2. Tylecote skied Spofforth to long-on. A boundary seemed likely, but Bonnor, in seven-league boots, sprinted thirty metres and took the catch at ankle height in a manner worthy of WG.

England seven for 97, and the captain came to the helm. Bligh was still looking for his first run when Bates, after another single, failed to get over a lifter from Horan and the spinning ball curled out to Murdoch at point. England was eight for 98 and in tatters.

George Studd played the first ball, from Spofforth, on to his own foot from which it bounced to Murdoch who had closed in. A general appeal for a catch was turned down by umpire Swift. Bligh took his first run when he drove Spofforth to long-on, then he prodded tentatively through a maiden from Horan. Turning Spofforth neatly to leg for a single, George Studd brought up the century. Getting forward, Bligh drove Spofforth towards the off boundary, but in the outer field, the ball dawdled and Bannerman prevented a boundary. Three more invaluable runs were accrued. On 8, Studd edged Spofforth and Garrett, in the slips, took a breathtakingly low catch — England nine for 115.

Morley came to share the wicket with his captain. Bligh was on 9 by now. Fortunately, he was on strike. Seizing what was probably his last opportunity, Bligh cut Horan for 4, then drove him straight for another boundary. He stepped out to the next two deliveries, missing both.

Spofforth, with his second attempt, took out Morley's leg stump and England was all out for 123. Australia was left with 152 for victory: that was the goal for tomorrow; right now, there was what was certain to be a torrid fifteen minutes' batting before stumps.

Bannerman was accompanied again by Giffen to the Australians' wicket where they faced the pace battery of Morley and Barlow. England's hopes of a quick breakthrough faded steadily as Morley hurled down four maidens to Giffen and Barlow swung three to the imperturbable Bannerman. At stumps, Australia was nought for nought.

Back in the pavilion, according to a paragraph buried deep in the *Age* newspaper the next morning, an allusion was made in conversation to Spofforth having cut up the wicket with his feet. 'This so annoyed the demon bowler that he struck at Mr Read of the English eleven. Fortunately for Spofforth, the genial Surrey secretary is as good tempered as he is muscular, and contented himself by smiling upon his ill-mannered adversary.'

The next morning was fine, and clear as a bell. Play began at 11 to be absolutely certain that, however slow the scoring might be, the match would be wrapped up that day. Although in the event the extra hour was not necessary, the early scoring rate suggested that it might well be.

Four maidens were reeled off before Bannerman saw a passage to the leg-side chains. Not to be outdone, Giffen cut Barlow in similar fashion, then flicked him to leg again for a couple more. Ten came up without loss, but the satisfaction that the 7000 spectators began to feel was shortlived. With 7 to his name, Giffen played over a half-volley from Barlow. Revolving bails flashed in the sunlight — Australia one for 11.

Percy McDonnell

Murdoch glanced Barlow for a single. The next from the Lancastrian lifted fiercely to perch for an instant on the shoulder of Bannerman's retreating bat and lob obligingly to the England skipper closing in rapidly from point. Australia was two for 12 and the first wave of uneasiness ran through the spectators with their faith in the home side.

Horan was fourth in. He took immediate command by cutting Barlow for 4. The ball jumped the fence. Then a single meant that he kept the bowling. He drove Morley for a single. Murdoch took the strike. Morley conjured from the turf an angry, red-eyed serpent that for an instant met Murdoch's gaze. The batsman dabbed. George Studd whooped. Most of the crowd groaned — Australia three for 18.

McDonnell also prodded at a venomous shooter from Morley — and this in turn flew straight to Bligh. The second nought recorded and Australia was four for 18.

87

Massie appeared at the crease. Two maidens. In trying to force Morley, Massie narrowly avoided giving the bowler a return catch. The next delivery, Massie aimed to sweep to leg. What actually happened Massie never really understood until told later, but he scrambled a couple as Bligh chased into the covers — 20 up.

Horan pushed Morley to short-leg for a single, then ran a bye as Tylecote was beaten by Barlow. A maiden to Morley. Barlow to Massie: 4 to long-off, 4 to backward square-leg. Morley to Horan, and a single brought up 30. Wild cheering for every stroke. More cheering as Horan, on 8, drove Barlow past mid-off and galloped towards the opposite stumps. Sheer disbelief by the spectators as Massie stood his ground. Both batsmen were at one end.

Australia five for 30, and the villainous Massie continued with 10. Bonnor and Massie now. Could these two hit their way to salvation? Hope for Australia still struggled. Bonnor quickly put a couple to his name with a single from Barlow and another glanced from Morley. These won the response normally accorded to boundaries. Massie clobbered Barlow towards long-off, but Read prevented his running more than a single. Again Massie whirled on Barlow. Everybody lost sight of the ball — that was except for George Studd who cuddled it joyfully to him in the slips.

Australia six for 33. Massie, with 11, was booed until he disappeared into the pavilion. His was a wicket thrown away. Sanity emerged in the form of John McCarthy Blackham, wicket-keeper second to none and a much-respected batsman. From the start he let the ball come to him, spending its venom, and consequently had time that the others, in their anxiety, had denied themselves. Stroking patiently to both sides of the wicket, he found rewarding gaps — for singles, a couple of pairs, and a brilliant 4 off his toes from Barlow to bring the total to 50. Bonnor, apparently tamed on this occasion by the burden of responsibility, had lashed out only once, reaping 3.

Blackham survived an lbw appeal. With 56 on the board, however, the wicket was persuaded by Barlow to conspire with him in outwitting Bonnor. The big man went down the wrong line to a shooter and this took his off stump. Australia was seven for 56 and Bonnor had made an uncharacteristically cautious 8.

There was Spofforth now to Blackham's support. Blackham hit Morley uncompromisingly hard but uppishly towards long-off. Read sprinted desperately, but the ball grounded fractionally beyond his grasp. Two more to Blackham.

Spofforth's first 2 came by hitting Barlow over the bowler's head. He repeated the stroke for 2 more. Each time, Barlow twisted round forlornly.

Blackham also cut Barlow for 2. Soon after this, Tylecote appealed for the stumping of his counterpart and was astounded to be rejected by umpire Elliott.

Spofforth stroked Morley in the opposite direction to that he intended. George Studd leapt and, this time, missed. In Barlow's next over, Spofforth charged him and connected, but Steel was able to manoeuvre under the ball at long-off and was applauded for the graceful manner in which he took it. The Demon departed with 7—Australia eight for 72.

With Palmer now in support, Blackham put Barlow to short-leg for a single. Two more byes were added as Palmer resorted rather desperately to employment of his pads. Blackham, picking a rare true ball from Barlow, middled for a fine off drive and the batsmen sprinted 3. Three maidens were spent before Palmer drove Morley to long-off for a couple—80 up.

Barlow now excited some vicious late turn and an inside edge from Blackham helped to collapse the stumps—Australia nine for 80.

Garrett came for the last stand with the England bowlers rampant. Two maidens. Two byes run. Barlow sent down a wide. His next effort, however, put Garrett's stumps in orbit. A 69-run victory had restored England's cricketing pride and, the *Age* noted, recovered the revered Ashes.

The hero of the hour was Richard Barlow with seven for 40 from 34·2 overs, including twenty maidens. Morley had bowled the rest—35 overs with nineteen maidens and two wickets for 34. Australia's top scorer in the second innings was Blackham with 26. Massie, with 11, was the only other batsman to reach double figures.

CHAPTER 8

Bolstered by their victory and consequent 'recovery' of the Ashes on the afternoon of 30 January 1883, Ivo Bligh and his merry men set sail the same evening for Queensland. They were scheduled to play two matches—in Brisbane against Eighteen of Queensland and at Maryborough against Eighteen of Maryborough.

In Brisbane on 2 and 3 February, heavy rain damaged the wicket to England's advantage. Before the rain came, Read made 84, his highest score in Australia. The top scorer for Queensland was Strickland who carried his bat in the first innings for 10. The tourists won by an innings and 154 runs.

There was rain, too, at Maryborough on 8 and 9 February. Again the Englishmen won—this time by an innings and 58 runs, but after an abysmal start to the batting with Bligh, Barlow, Bates, and Steel all out for a total of 5, Read (66) and George Studd (43) performed the rescue. Maryborough, in its first innings, was nine for 19 and the second time round, nine for 14.

The tourists then returned to Sydney for what has become recognised as *the* Test match. In this encounter, Bligh's side came up against an XI representing the current available full strength of Australia, as opposed to William Murdoch's side which toured England in 1882 and, against most expectations, brought off that astonishing victory at Kennington Oval.

In fact, the strengthened Australian XI was predominantly of those who had been to England. Murdoch still had the captaincy. McDonnell would have been included, but was not available. Excluded were Garrett and Massie. Henry Scott, a first choice from Victoria, was ill. Into the vacancies stepped Evans, Midwinter, and Harry Boyle. At The Oval the previous August, Boyle had sewn up one end while, at the other, Spofforth had cried 'Havoc!'

Edwin Evans, of New South Wales, was a round-arm spin bowler of great accuracy and in the 1870s accomplished much for his State in combination with Spofforth. He could also give a sting to a side's batting tail.

William Evans Midwinter was born in Gloucestershire. He played for that county and, after emigrating, for the State of Victoria. He achieved the unique distinction of playing both for and against Australia. In 1878, while touring England with the Australian side, he had been virtually kidnapped by W. G. Grace to play for Gloucestershire against Surrey at The Oval. Midwinter was a medium-pace bowler who could spin the ball a lot and he was a steady right-handed batsman, comfortable in the middle order.

Ivo Bligh won the toss for the third time in succession and elected to bat. Gusting winds from the south were pushing dark clouds across the Moore Park ground. Rain was yet again in the offing as Murdoch led out his team in the wake of umpires Swift and Elliott. The Australian skipper put himself as usual at point, Bannerman at mid-on, Bonnor short slip, Spofforth long slip,

90

William Midwinter

Harry Boyle

Horan long leg, Boyle mid-on, Evans cover point, Giffen long-on, and Midwinter at short-leg.

Barlow and Charlie Studd were the openers for England. The play began with Palmer from the southern end bowling right-arm, medium pace to the Lancashire stalwart, Richard Barlow. Facing good line and length from virtually the first delivery, the professional was satisfied to let a maiden be registered. Palmer was complemented from the northern end by Midwinter, another medium-pace right-hander. The second delivery from Midwinter left Studd groping and brought an appeal from Blackham behind the stumps. Studd survived this to cut the last of the over neatly for England's first 2 runs. Aided by the breeze, Palmer sent down his second maiden. Midwinter again, and Studd, his footwork suggestive of ballet, turned neatly on his toes to leg for a couple more.

There were two more maidens before Barlow's first scoring stroke—driving Palmer to mid-off for 2. Another four maidens reflected the accuracy of the bowling, sharp fielding, and the solidly defensive attitude of the batsmen. Studd broke the succession of maidens by cutting Midwinter through the slips for 2 and then driving him to long-off so hard and fast that there was time only to take a single. Against Palmer now, Studd flashed for the first boundary, just forward of point. Midwinter to Barlow who had been under siege virtually from the start. Extra lift found an edge and Murdoch proved equal to the fleeting chance. Barlow's 2 had taken half an hour and England was one for 13.

Leslie saw out the over. Studd cut Palmer past point's left hand for a single and Leslie's first runs were 2 to leg. Midwinter slanted in another maiden. Palmer, pitching shorter and faster, was edged through the slips by Leslie. Four—and a total of 20. A maiden from Midwinter to Studd, then Leslie put Palmer comfortably to leg for a pair. In the first bowling change, Palmer was rested for Spofforth. The crowd stirred eagerly. The last ball of the Demon's first over caught Studd in two minds and fizzed outside the off-stump to be clawed down by Blackham. Leslie, from deep in his shell, pecked at Midwinter.

The brothers Studd: Kynaston, Charles, and George. Kynaston never played Test cricket

Keen fielding by Evans prevented a boundary when Leslie darted at Spofforth. Evans was in the action again to deal with two Studd off-drives, each of which yielded 3, making 9 in all from the over. Midwinter restricted Leslie to a single and Boyle relieved the expensive Spofforth. Leslie edged Boyle's first into the slips, but a dazzling right-handed stop by Bonnor denied him even a single. The third delivery streaked from an edge and

Bonnor turned a hard chance into an easy-looking catch. Leslie had made 17 with some attractive and confident strokes under great pressure.

England two for 37, and Charlie Studd, on 11, was joined by Steel who pushed the last of the over back along the pitch with a gentle consideration that suggested the ball might be made of porcelain.

Studd was caged again by Midwinter. During Boyle's next over, also a maiden, Steel moved to the pitch and watched anxiously as the ball landed just short of Murdoch's left hand. Forty came up when Studd drove Midwinter for 2 and then one. Steel found his first pair by turning Midwinter to leg. In Midwinter's next over, Steel would have been run out had the bowler taken cleanly a return to the stumps. At lunch, England was two for 48.

In the afternoon, Sammy Jones substituted for Giffen who had strained a knee a few days previously. This had become troublesome again. Studd brought up the 50 when there was a rare moment of indecision in the field. Although Midwinter kept one end virtually sewn up—at one stage he bowled six successive maidens—both batsmen made runs steadily from the other, 60 and 70 being duly recorded. Palmer came back when 80 was hoisted and Midwinter was rested for Horan. The Irishman was immediately hooked for 4 and driven for 2 by Studd. Steel worked the ball regularly on both sides and the century was reached when Studd took a single from Horan.

A leg bye was next and then Steel late cut Palmer for 4 and swept the next to leg for another boundary. With the total on 110, Steel drove to mid-off. Studd started down the wicket, then, realising the futility of his action, turned back—too late. A smart underhand return from Midwinter shattered the stumps for the third wicket. Studd had contributed his highest Test score to date with 48.

Read, fresh from his 84 in Brisbane, came to Steel's support. With the total still on 110, Steel edged Evans' spin, but Bonnor, in the slips, dropped it. Three singles came in rapid succession. Read seemed happy to let Steel set the pace. The scoring rate became brisk. With 130 up, Spofforth came back. Read hit the Demon's second delivery to the boundary and his third for a single. The last of the over, Steel cut to the fence.

Steel, by now, was punishing all-comers with his awesome cuts and off-drives. This partnership had produced 40 and the total was 150 when Read, on 11, obliged Boyle with an edge and this one was gobbled by Bonnor at slip.

Tylecote was next to Steel's support and he saw off Boyle. Steel pushed Spofforth into the covers for a single. Tylecote, with sweet timing, turned the Demon to leg for 4 and cut the next for a single. Facing Boyle again, Tylecote, on 5, was beaten by one that kept low. He was the first of the innings to be clean bowled and England was five for 156.

Steel awaited Barnes and then cut the Demon for a single. Barnes eagerly cut Spofforth for 2 and then carelessly unleashed himself at a bailer.

England six for 159. Steel, on 67, now watched Bates' arrival at the crease. The Yorkshireman eventually got off the mark by late-cutting Boyle for a couple. An overthrow brought up 170. Steel then drove Spofforth to the long-on boundary, but then almost played on in clumsily late-cutting the next. Midwinter had just completed another good-looking maiden when, at 4.40, the rain, for so long a threat, was driven across the ground by great gusts of wind. Umbrellas blossomed as the players sprinted off.

In only five minutes, however, it was fine again for Steel, now on 83, to continue along his glory trail. Midwinter took some punishment before Steel's progress was again delayed by the downfall of his partner. Bates lofted Midwinter to a spot at long-on where Bonnor, with huge strides and hands, arrived to take a spectacular catch above and behind his head — his third catch of the innings. Bates had hammered 9 and England was seven for 199.

Bligh was applauded to the wicket and patiently negotiated a maiden from Boyle. Midwinter again to Steel. As the Lancashire amateur cut immaculately for 2, the applause burst for England's total reaching 200 and Steel's own century. Facing Midwinter again, Bligh blazed into the covers. Murdoch got some fingers there, but failed to hold on — even so, the batsman decided not to risk anything. Not long after, Bligh at last succeeded in forcing wide of point and ran 2, but one of these was judged to be short.

Going forward at every opportunity, Bligh peppered the long field. When Palmer overpitched slightly, the England captain rattled the fence in front of the packed grandstand. He cut Palmer for 2 more, and then put Spofforth away for 2 and to long-off for 4 more. When he was on 19, however, Bligh went over the top of a yorker from Palmer and was bowled — England eight for 236.

Steel's fifth partner of the day was George Studd. The Cambridge all-rounder saw Spofforth and Palmer put to the boundary and 4 more byes on the total before himself driving Palmer to long-off for 3. This was George Studd's first and last scoring stroke. He was run out in attempting a second run for Steel. Credit for a brilliant return went to Bannerman. England was nine for 263 at stumps on the first day.

The next morning was fresh and fine. With the last ball of his first over, Palmer bowled England's last man, Fred Morley, for nought. Steel, denied the opportunity of adding to his overnight tally, remained unbeaten on 135.

At 12.15, the pride of Sydney, little Alec Bannerman, walked out to a fresh wicket with his new opening partner, the towering George Bonnor. This pair's contrasting statures were appreciated by the cheerful crowd. Amid fading laughter, the pair prepared for the task ahead. Bannerman took first strike against Barlow from the northern end. George Studd was at mid-off, Charlie Studd third man, Leslie long-off, Steel forward cover, Morley short leg, Bates mid-on, Barnes short slip, Read at leg slip, Bligh at point, and Tylecote behind the stumps.

Bannerman struck the second delivery for a single and Bonnor turned the next off his legs for 2. Morley bowled the first maiden, Barlow the second, and Morley the third. Bannerman then amazed everyone by skying Barlow into the covers. Steel made a valiant effort, but never really had the opportunity to position himself for a cruel chance and the batsmen crossed 3 times. Retaining the strike, Bannerman late cut the next delivery, from Morley, for 3 more. In his next over, Morley sent down his fastest delivery yet. It flashed past Tylecote down the leg side for 4 byes.

Bonnor, with some surprisingly delicate strokes for him, quickly accumulated 5. Bannerman got an unexpected boundary when Read lost sight of a ball turned to leg and worth only a single. An even share of the strike and scoring strokes brought up 30, but with only one more added, Bannerman got too much under Morley and the ball flew to Barlow in the slips. He had made an unusual 10, exciting enough in its way to maintain chatter until the fall of the next wicket.

Australia was one for 31 and Murdoch made his entrance. Before the total advanced, Bonnor cut Barlow high to cover point. Steel brought it down, but failed to hold. Murdoch worked cautiously through a maiden from Barlow who was keeping immaculate line and length. Morley served up a maiden to Bonnor and then Murdoch, oddly nervous, was clean bowled by Barlow without having scored.

Australia was two for 34, and there was more than enough for the crowd to chatter about.

Horan came into the firing line. After a leg bye, the newcomer put Morley to leg for a couple and Barlow for a neat single.

Bonnor suddenly had some trouble in coping with Barlow and was glad to settle for another maiden. Horan managed a single from each bowler, but the Irishman, in going forward to Morley, lost his grip on his bat. The ball went up to George Studd who was prowling around point.

Australia was three for 39 and far from happy. The wicket looked friendly enough, but obviously had a darker side, too. Giffen hobbled out, accompanied by Murdoch to act as his runner. The sight of them did not inspire much confidence and the crowd settled more quietly. Barlow contained Bonnor and three maidens were recorded before Bonnor, handling his bat like a matchstick, cut Barlow through the slips to the boundary—40 on the board.

Giffen, showing more freedom of movement than was generally expected of him, went to the pitch of Barlow and the ball went blazing through the covers for his first boundary. The crowd warmed to Giffen. Morley again to Bonnor and a soft chance, but Steel, for the third time, failed to complete the dismissal of the big fellow. Seven, in all, were then taken from the over. Giffen chalked up another boundary from Barlow just before lunch.

The afternoon session began with a maiden from Morley to Bonnor who was continuing despite some stomach trouble. Giffen put Barlow through the slips for 2. Morley pounded in again with a short one that lifted nastily. It soared from Bonnor's bat to point where Bligh touched it, but it still managed to elude him. Another Barlow maiden to Giffen and then Bonnor collected 2 more in driving Morley to long-off. Giffen pushed Barlow for a single past mid-off and manoeuvred through another aggressive maiden from Morley. There was applause for Bonnor's skill in turning Barlow to leg for 3. Three more maidens before Giffen swung Barlow for a splendid boundary to long-off. The total was 70. Morley added to Bonnor's discomfort by rapping him on the knuckles. After a maiden from Barlow, Bonnor lashed out in more familiar fashion, mishit Morley, but nevertheless secured 4. Eighty appeared on the scoreboard when Bonnor again lashed Morley, much more soundly this time, but only for 3. Barnes took over from Barlow and Bonnor drove the Nottinghamshire man's first and third deliveries for two each.

In the next over from Barnes, Bonnor lifted high but safely and ran 4 as the ball finally dawdled towards the boundary and was snatched up just short of it. These runs brought up Bonnor's 50 for which he was roundly applauded. His incredible luck had contributed to some great entertainment.

Australia was now again in the nervous 90s and, accordingly, the run rate fell away. Morley sweated through another maiden. Bonnor cut Barnes for a single. Morley banged in another fine maiden. Giffen drove Barnes for 2 and put him through the slips for 3. One needed for the century.

Bates came on for Morley and immediately bowled a maiden. Barnes to Bonnor again — and Tylecote at the wicket missed an edge. Another maiden from Bates. Barnes to Bonnor, a loose one down the off side. Bonnor stepped back and carved to the boundary. The crowd erupted to greet the hundred. This roar had hardly died when Bonnor rattled the pavilion fence — at the expense of Barnes — to trigger off more delight.

In the next over, Bonnor gained yet another life after being dropped by Barlow off Bates. The next delivery was thundered to the boundary. Leslie came on for Barnes and, with the last delivery of a maiden over, was unlucky not to have Giffen stumped. During his next over, Leslie sent down a wide, but then induced Giffen to drive uppishly into the covers where George Studd, dropping to one knee, took the catch at cover point.

Australia was four for 113. Giffen, with Murdoch in his shadow, departed, having made a thoroughly entertaining 27.

Bonnor's new associate at the wicket was Midwinter. Morley came back for Bates and sent down another maiden. Midwinter soon glanced Leslie to leg for 2 and Bonnor did similarly. Leslie bowled another wide, then Midwinter cut him very late through the slips to the boundary. The scoreboard showed 120. A maiden from Morley and 3 more to Midwinter off Leslie. Bonnor jabbed Morley into the covers for 2. The erratic Leslie was taken off and Barlow came back. Midwinter, on 10, went over his second delivery, and walked without a glance at his splayed stumps.

Australia was five for 128 and the stage was now set for the Blackham–Bonnor partnership. Blackham took a quick single from Barlow, then appeared to turn the same bowler to leg, but after 3 were run, umpire Elliott signalled 3 leg byes. Morley extracted some vicious lift and turn and Bonnor spent some time nursing fingers that were already badly bruised. He retaliated by hammering 7 from the next three deliveries. He went on the

Jack Blackham

rampage again minutes later, skying Barlow to long-on where, unbelievably, Steel dropped Bonnor for the fourth time. Blackham skied in the same direction, but this dropped much sooner and nobody was able to get near. There was applause for the 150, but Australia was still 112 behind. Two more maidens were fenced through before Blackham broke out again, pulling Morley for 4. Bonnor was on 87 when there was a break for drinks. During the pause, umpire Elliott authorised that Blackham be credited with the earlier 3 leg byes. Morley was rested. Steel was the new bowler and after being hit for 3 by Blackham, he had the consolation of having Bonnor caught in the slips by Barlow without addition to his score. Bonnor had had eight lives—at 5, 17, 24, 30, 31, 52, 61, and 82. Australia was six for 160.

Blackham was now the mainstay. After being joined by Palmer, he cut Barlow beautifully to the boundary. Palmer, before scoring, put Steel up to point where Bligh was pleased to take a comfortable catch—Australia seven for 164.

What would Evans do? A leg bye was run and before Evans could do anything much, he was missed in the slips by Barnes off Barlow. Stepping out, Blackham thrashed powerfully at both Steel and Barlow. His intention now was clearly to get runs quickly while he could. Soon 180 was showing. At 190, Morley was put back in the attack and promptly bowled a maiden to Evans, but Blackham, less easily subdued, kept on the run trail. Charlie Studd came on and Blackham soon hammered him for 2 to bring up 200. Blackham by now boasted 42. The bats continued to flash and the ball travelled regularly to each side of the wicket. There was a wholesome swell of applause for Blackham's 50. Soon after this, Bates was tried and Blackham, in lunging at a full toss, lost the line and his bails.

Australia was eight for 220 to which Blackham had contributed an invaluable flawless 57.

Evans was on 13 when Spofforth took the crease. The Demon, showing urgency, cut Bates for a single and retained the strike against Steel. Before Spofforth could score again, Steel made one rear, find an edge, and spin to Bates at slip—Australia nine for 221.

Steel again—to the last man, Boyle, who pushed safely to short leg. Several maidens were now relieved only by singles gleaned from the intervening overs. Boyle eventually disrupted this tempo by slamming Bates to the boundary. The scoreboard showed 230. Barlow returned and bowled a maiden to Evans. Boyle heaved Steel for 2, then tapped and ran for a cheeky single. More smart singles brought the total to 240. Barnes took over from Steel and bowled a maiden. More singles, a couple, then Boyle cut Barnes for 3 and at stumps Australia was nine for 248 with Evans and Boyle both on 20. The home side still needed 14 to avoid a first innings deficit.

During Monday night, there was rain. Dawn was fine, however, but the threat of rain hung about. The turf was still damp when play resumed. Evans and Boyle were cheered to the wicket. Boyle took first strike. Barlow bowled a maiden from the northern end. From the south end, Bates sent down a maiden to Evans. From Barlow's next offering, Boyle picked a single and there was a bye which brought the total to 250. Two more byes came and a single as Evans snicked Bates to leg.

Three were run when Boyle cut Bates dangerously late. Barlow to Boyle — a maiden. Evans cut Bates for 1 and Boyle took a similar liberty for 2. Bates again, and Boyle cut him powerfully behind point for 3. One more run would put the sides exactly level. Barlow pitched just outside the off stump and, just a little too eagerly, Boyle swung while neglecting to move his feet properly. George Studd, in his favourite position at mid-off, stretched upwards and to his right for a fine catch — Australia all out 262.

Boyle had made 29, Evans was unbeaten with 22. Steel had taken three for 24, Barlow three for 88, Morley two for 45, Leslie one for 11, and Bates one for 24. England had a lead of 1 and the match was wide open.

A new wicket awaited Barlow and Studd. From the north end, it was Spofforth who took issue with Barlow. The Lancastrian cracked into the covers for 2. Boyle provided medium pace from the south end. He was aided by a strengthening wind. The last ball of his first over was pushed square by Studd for a single. The same batsman took a single from Spofforth. Boyle bowled his first maiden. Spofforth conceded a single to Barlow and was cut by Studd to the chains for the first boundary of the day. Barlow's next single made the total 10. Studd clipped another single from Boyle and rocketed Spofforth for 4. The next went for a single. Barlow hammered each bowler for 2. With 20 put rapidly on the board, the openers had rid themselves of most of the close fielders.

Studd narrowly avoided being run out when he underestimated the speed at which Bannerman was able to return. Spofforth was replaced by Palmer who, in his second over, was thundered to the long-on boundary by Studd who was getting to the pitch of almost everything — 30 up. At last, Studd missed in heaving at Boyle. Blackham dazzled in taking the bails off, but Studd's back foot had never left home. At lunch, England was 43 without loss. Studd was on 24 and Barlow 15.

The first four overs of the afternoon yielded 1 run. Barlow was hit on the side by Palmer and there was a delay until the batsman had recovered. With the total at 51, Midwinter came into the attack and began with a maiden. Four more maidens were sent down before Studd, on 31 by this time, tried to force Midwinter, but succeeded only in putting the ball up to Murdoch at short leg — England one for 54.

Leslie came to the wicket. Barlow eased Palmer for a single, but then, without good cause, chased a rare loose one from Midwinter and was caught by Bonnor in the slips. He had made 20.

England two for 55, and Steel took guard. Would he continue to sparkle? He was put to the test immediately with some furious swing and turn from Palmer and Midwinter. Leslie brought the total to 60 by twice forcing Midwinter for 2. Steel began with a single from each bowler. Leslie clouted Palmer for 4, 2, and then 2 more. At 77, Horan relieved Palmer. There was a roar as, with his first delivery, the Irishman skittled Leslie—England was three down.

Read took the vacant end and dealt carefully with the rest of Horan's over. Boyle returned but did not prevent a sudden flow of runs. Spofforth soon replaced Horan and Midwinter came back. With the total at 97, Palmer took over from Midwinter. Steel immediately dabbed Palmer through the slips for a single and then turned Spofforth to leg for a single. Spofforth lifted himself to deny the enemy 100, won that extra bit of turn and made Read play on. Read departed with 11. England was four for 99 and Tylecote headed for the crease.

It was Palmer who conceded the century, Steel flicking him to leg for a single. This put the newcomer on strike, but Tylecote never actually struck the ball because the next delivery bowled him—England five for 100.

Bates took up the cause. Steel took a single from Spofforth and 2 from Palmer. Bates snicked Spofforth through the slips to the boundary. The Demon's next effort, very fast, beat the bat and wicketkeeper and bounded away for 4 byes. After adding another couple, Steel fell to the Demon— cleaned bowled for 21.

England six for 112 and Bates awaited the arrival at the wicket of his captain. The scoring was halted as the new and fragile partnership steered through six maidens. Bates eventually took a single from Palmer and very soon after this, another off Spofforth. He cut Palmer for 3 and pushed for 1. At last Bligh ended a torrid period at the crease by turning Spofforth to leg for 3 and was further encouraged as Bates blasted the Demon through the covers to the fence. The Yorkshireman attempted to deal with the last ball of the over in the same manner—and was dropped by Murdoch at point.

Bligh brought up 130 as he belted Spofforth to the leg boundary. At 136, Spofforth was rested. Horan took the ball. He did nothing much with his first delivery, but succeeded with the last of the over when Bligh, on 10, tried to savage him. This time Murdoch, at point, successfully held an infinitely more difficult catch. England was seven for 137.

Barnes was next to provide support. Bates kept the total climbing at a fair rate with couples and singles from both bowlers. Barnes edged Palmer for 2 to leg and pushed a single to the off. A bye brought up 150. Barnes struck Palmer to square-leg for 4 and Bates twice hit Horan for 2. Murdoch was prompted to bring back Midwinter for Palmer. Barnes took 3 from his first over. Spofforth was thrown into the assault again. Bates soon cut the Demon to the boundary and Midwinter fared little better against Barnes. The total was 177 when Murdoch made a double bowling change to create the combination of Palmer and Boyle. Barnes added only a single, for 20, when he put one uppishly straight back to Boyle—England eight for 178.

George Studd approached the wicket briskly and slammed the first from Boyle forward of point for 3. He continued to test the field with some powerful shots. Bates scorched Boyle to the long-off boundary. In Boyle's next over, Studd whirled on him, but failed to get the necessary height.

100

Murdoch took his second blistering catch at point. Studd had made nine and England was nine for 192.

Morley came out to form the last partnership. He made a vigorous start by driving Boyle into the covers for 2. Bates took 3 more off Palmer before Boyle had Morley caught at the wicket by Blackham with only a few minutes to stumps. Palmer, Midwinter, Spofforth, Boyle, and Horan had each taken two wickets, Palmer's cost being 59 and Horan's 15.

Australia needed 199 for a victory which would square the series.

To the relief of the Australians, the next day was fine, although Sydney was buffeted by a southerly gale. The wicket at the north end was difficult at first, but improved after the first half hour and both ends played well for the remaining hours of the match. This time, Bannerman had Murdoch as his opening partner on the fourth and final wicket. Some 15 000 spectators saw Bannerman take first strike from Bates who started from the south end. The second delivery was turned to leg for 2, George Studd collecting well. The next went in the same direction and beat George Studd to rebound from the fence. It was an auspicious start and much out of character for the Sydney man. Was Bannerman making a special effort to entertain his home crowd? Murdoch obviously had no such inclination as he cautiously fended off Barlow. A leg bye resulted and brought the Australian captain into line with Bates — for another maiden over. Bannerman pushed Barlow past mid-off for a single. Each bowler sent down a maiden.

Bates again, and an edge from Bannerman was into and out of Tylecote's hands before the spectators appreciated what had happened — but the other England players did and were appalled by the chance gone begging.

Bannerman launched into his second life by driving the unlucky Bates to long-on for 2. Three maidens were bowled before the next run came — a single to Bannerman off Bates. Two more maidens had gone down before Bates conceded another single to Bannerman. Four more maidens and then Bannerman jabbed one from Barlow and saw out another maiden from Bates. Barlow kept Murdoch pinned down. Bannerman cut first Bates for a single and then Barlow to short leg for the same. Next he drove Bates for 1 and cut Barlow attractively for 2. After battling for forty minutes, Murdoch indulged himself by pushing Bates for a single to earn some pockets of cheering. He took another maiden from Barlow. Bannerman could find no scope with Bates and Murdoch once more prodded ineffectually at Barlow. Bannerman drove Bates and the total staggered to 20. Bannerman had 18, Murdoch 1, and there was that leg bye — this after forty-five minutes.

Murdoch, apparently beginning to feel safer, cut Barlow for 2. Bates tried a long hop. Bannerman chopped a single and again found it impossible to make anything of Barlow.

Morley was given the ball. Murdoch worked the fast man's third delivery for a single. Barlow sent down his usual maiden. Bannerman had difficulty with the lift from Morley. Murdoch middled Barlow. Morley misfielded and the ball reached the boundary — just. Twice more, Murdoch drove Barlow for

101

2, the first stroke bringing up 30. After a maiden from Morley to Bannerman, Leslie replaced Barlow. During the seventh successive maiden, Leslie bowled 2 wides. After Morley bowled the eighth maiden, the England players gathered round Bligh for a discussion lasting a couple of minutes. When they broke up, Steel replaced Leslie and bowled a maiden to Murdoch. Bannerman glanced Morley for a single. Two more maidens. Bannerman drove Steel to long-on for 4. Charlie Studd relieved Morley and bowled a maiden to Bannerman. Murdoch took a single off Steel, as did Bannerman. Studd bowled a maiden to Bannerman. Lunch came with Bannerman on 22 and Murdoch on 13. Four byes made a total of 39 without loss. The gale blew the players into the pavilion.

The first over of the afternoon was a maiden from Steel to Murdoch, but a leg bye brought up 40. Murdoch cut Bates for 2 and Bannerman played a maiden from Steel. Murdoch steered Bates to mid-off for a single. A maiden from Steel, a maiden from Bates and Murdoch drove Steel for a single.

Then Bates moved one off the wicket which Murdoch just tickled. Barlow scooped at slip. Murdoch had made a painfully careful 17 and Australia was one for 44.

Bonnor came out, challenging the gale. Bannerman took another maiden from Steel. Bonnor soon got applause by cutting Bates for 3. Fifty went up when Bannerman cut the next ball for 4, but Bonnor lunged at Steel, mistimed and looped the ball to George Studd at forward cover — Australia two for 51.

Horan came and drove the second delivery from Bates straight back into the bowler's hands — Australia three for 51. England was reviving.

Giffen appeared, again with Murdoch to run for him. Bannerman was cheered when he drove Steel straight for 3. Bates then bowled a maiden and Giffen opened his score with a grand drive from Steel for which there was no need even to begin to run. The next delivery went the same way, but Leslie prevented a boundary. Three were run.

A maiden to Bates. Barlow relieved Steel after another conference. Immediately, Barlow sent down a maiden to Bannerman. Giffen could do nothing with Bates, but Bannerman carved Barlow for 2. Three byes from Bates' next over to Giffen sent up 70.

Eighty came with surprising rapidity. Giffen hammered Barlow to the pavilion fence. Bannerman blazed Bates for 3 and got a bonus couple from an overthrow. The run-starved crowd roared its pleasure. Another boundary to Bannerman and another to Giffen. The 100 sprang up with 3 to Bannerman off Bates.

George Studd was brought on to try to stem the flood and Bannerman, on 63, obligingly drove his first delivery to the England captain at point. Australia was four for 107 and England was still in with a fighting chance.

Blackham joined Giffen and the tempo eased again. Blackham was satisfied to start with singles and his first really ambitious stroke, making 3, brought up 120. The total continued mounting steadily and maidens were correspondingly fewer. Giffen saw the total to 130, Blackham to 140, and 150 was posted when Giffen turned Barnes to square-leg for 2. England again urgently needed wickets.

Blackham pulled Steel grandly for 2. There were 2 byes and then Blackham swung Steel cleanly to the chains. He cut a single from the last of the over. A new over from Barnes and immediately Blackham turned him square for 2. The rest of the over was unproductive.

Giffen went down the wicket to Steel, flayed, and missed. Tylecote, ball in hand, swooped on the stumps. Australia was five for 162 and Giffen had made a splendid 32. The England side clustered together urgently as Evans came to the crease. The gale blew down the stumps and the group broke up to chase bails.

Blackham hit Barnes, and then Steel, for a single each. Evans lofted Steel straight back over the bowler's head, too high for Barnes to do anything about, but the catch was easily taken by Leslie.

Australia was six for 160. The tourists conferred again. They needed four wickets, Australia required 39 runs. Blackham was the stumbling block for England. Midwinter took guard.

The batsmen resorted to ultra caution. Blackham eventually found another single and Midwinter began with a single. Blackham pushed for another. There was a leg bye off Barnes and then Blackham flashed Steel to the long-off boundary, causing the now hushed crowd to erupt. The wind snatched away both sets of bails.

Barlow came back and had his third delivery cut by Blackham for 3. Tremendous applause again. The next delivery from Steel went for a single. Steel also conceded one to Midwinter. Barlow conceded 2 to Midwinter.

Blackham defiantly drove Steel for 2, making his ground for the second only an instant before Tylecote sent the bails flying. The tense crowd let out an 'Aaaaah!'

Australia needed 7 for victory. Bates was given the ball in the hope that he could perform miracles with his last fling. He succeeded in pinning down Blackham. Barlow did similarly with Midwinter. The stumps at the south end were blown down again.

Yet another maiden seemed likely from Bates—until Blackham cut him for 3. Only another hat-trick from Bates in his next over was asked of him. Barlow again to Blackham—who advanced swinging. The ball streaked to the long-off boundary. Blackham, hero of the hour, was undefeated with 68. Midwinter was happy with 8 not out. Steel had taken three for 49, Bates two for 52, and Studd one for 8. Australia, with four wickets to spare, had squared the series.

CHAPTER 9

That same evening, Ivo Bligh and the other amateurs in the England side set off by train for Melbourne. The professionals followed a few days later.

On Friday, 9 March, the tourists began a match in Melbourne against the Victorian XI which included McDonnell, Blackham, Bonnor, Horan, Midwinter, Palmer, and Boyle. The captain, William Henry Cooper, a slow, right-arm, leg-break bowler, had made his Test debut at Melbourne in January 1882 when he took a total of nine wickets for 200 in 98·2 overs. His great-grandson is Paul Sheahan who played for Australia from 1968 to 1972.

Patrick George McShane was a left-hand bowler who later played in three Tests. Doctor Henry James Herbert Scott, a right-handed batsman, had been unlucky not to be in the fourth Test. Later, he toured England twice, as captain in 1886. E. Turner was the only member of the side never involved in Anglo-Australian Test cricket. Fred Morley was not well enough to play for the tourists.

On Saturday, play ended at 5 because the wicket was flooded by rain. The outcome of the match, on the Monday, was a win for Victoria by an innings and 73 runs. This was England's only beating by a State side, but the most crushing defeat of the tour.

The next day, Tuesday, 13 March 1883 — which happened to be Ivo Bligh's twenty-fourth birthday — the Melbourne Cricket Club gave a farewell banquet for the English cricketers. The dinner was held in the pavilion which was decorated with flags, flowers, and ferns.

The Melbourne Cricket Club chairman, Mr F. G. Smith, expressed apologies on behalf of the club president, Sir William Clarke, who was unavoidably absent. When some months ago (continued Mr Smith, according to the *Age* newspaper) they met in the pavilion to welcome Mr Bligh and his comrades, they all formed most pleasurably anticipations of the coming cricket. He, at any rate, had. He thought they would all agree with him that their guests had never been surpassed by any team who had preceded them. They had shown the most perfect cricket, and also equanimity under defeat and moderation in victory (applause).

They were the pleasantest of pleasant men. Their genial cordiality was first apparent in that pavilion, and since then it had been seen everywhere. He had to express the gratification of the Melbourne Cricket Club at the visit of the present team. Mr Bligh had done everything in his power towards falling in with their arrangements and had thus effectually aided them in bringing a difficult enterprise to a successful issue. He congratulated Mr Bligh and his team on the success that had attended their efforts to regain what had been spoken of as the 'ashes' of English cricket. They were now only to be won again in England. Australians might repeat their exploits on the English cricket field, and their doing so might be the means of bringing their guests of that evening back again. They had become honorary members of the Melbourne Cricket Club and had accepted a badge, which, when they wore it, would cause them to remember that pavilion. He proposed 'Our Guests.'

The toast was drunk, amid musical honours, the band playing 'Nelly Bligh,' which caused much laughter.

Mr Bligh, on rising to respond, was received with a perfect storm of applause, which lasted for some time.

He (Mr Bligh) thanked them on behalf of the team for the extremely kind

The statue of Sir William Clarke in Melbourne, Victoria

manner in which they had received the toast. He could hardly find words to express his feelings, especially on hearing the familiar tune played by the band. At the early part of their tour, he had expressed the opinion that they were an unlucky team, and he now thought that having had a man with a broken rib playing with them during the whole tour was really bad luck. They could not fail to admire this man's pluck (applause). He had the audacity on the occasion of a previous dinner which had been given to them, to say that they had come here to beard the kangaroo on his own ground. Four months had now passed, and yet that kangaroo seemed to hop as jauntily as ever.

Regarding those 'ashes' of England cricket, he thought the best thing that could be done with them would be to bury them in some corner of the Melbourne Cricket Ground (laughter). The team did not talk much of the last match, but he thought their retrospect generally was a most pleasant one. Little differences would arise in matches contested like theirs had been, but those that had happened were not worth mentioning. The matches in Australia were the best they had ever played. They had come 16 000 miles to get the opportunity of playing Spofforth on a dry wicket, but had been disappointed. The wickets they could have had at home were quite as dry. He wished to thank the Press for the fair and impartial way in which they had been treated. The public also had always been impartial, as much so as they ever were in England.

The team would be glad to meet an Australian eleven in England, and be more glad to beat them. He took that last opportunity of thanking everyone who had been so kind to them during their stay here, especially the Melbourne Cricket Club and Mr Alexander who had acted as their manager for most of the time. Most of the members of the team would be leaving shortly, but one or two, including himself, were going to stay a little longer. Before he sat down, he had much pleasure in proposing 'Success to the Melbourne Club,' and coupling with this toast the name of the vice-president, Mr F. Grey Smith.

The chairman responded and in the course of his remarks stated that the club had now reached the maximum number of members allowed by its rules. He also stated that the committee had presented a gold locket, commemorative of their visit, to the professional members of the team.

Mr Barlow responded on behalf of himself and his brother professionals.

Mr Bligh proposed 'The Victorious Victorian Eleven' with which he coupled the name of their captain, Mr W. H. Cooper. Mr Cooper suitably replied, and the company soon afterwards separated . . .

By the time Ivo Bligh sailed for home some days after the rest of the team, the Clarkes' music teacher, Florence Morphy, had agreed to marry him.

During the England summer of 1883, Ivo played in a few matches for Kent and Cobham, but illness prevented more appearances. In the early autumn of that year he sailed again for Australia and back to Florence. This voyage apparently passed without incident.

106

A NOVELTY.

Diminutive Masher (from neighbouring colony—who is given to drawing odious comparisons between his own city and Melbourne—to his partner).—"WHY DO YOU MELBOURNE PEOPLE USE PROGRAMMES FOR SMALL DANCES LIKE THIS? WE NEVER DO."

Young Lady.—"DON'T YOU? WHAT DO YOU USE THEN?"

Diminutive Masher.—"OH! WE USE OUR HEADS."

Young Lady.—"DO YOU, REALLY? WHAT A VERY GOOD IDEA. I HAVE HEARD OF GENTLEMEN USING THEIR SHIRTCUFFS, BUT I *never* HEARD OF THEM USING THEIR HEADS BEFORE."

ENGLAND V. AUSTRALIA.—ANOTHER "MATCH."

THE ENGLISH CRICKETER OVER THERE AND THE VICTORIAN MAIDEN OVER HERE.

AIR : *Nelly Bligh.*

IVO BLIGH
Heaved a sigh,
　　When across the main,
Said—" Unto Victoria's shores
　　I'll go back again."
Hi Ivo! Ho Ivo!
　　Cupid takes a turn,
Puts to Ivo's heart his torch,
　　And "Ivo's ashes" burn.

Ivo Bligh's
Roguish eyes
　　Make a sudden "catch,"
Sees a Southern beauty here,
　　And seeks to play a "match."
Hi Ivo! Ho Ivo!
　　The phœnix is the same,
From his "ashes" he will rise
　　To play the same old game.

Ivo Bligh
Means to try
　　A life of married bliss,
Let's hope that it will be a "hit,"
　　Although he seeks a "miss."

Hi Ivo! Ho Ivo!
　　Happy may you be!
May bad luck never "run you out '
　　From your felicity.

Ivo Bligh
Need not cry
　　For cricket's ashes more,
Since he takes his flame away
　　To burn on England's shore.
Hi Ivo! Ho Ivo!
　　This truth never doubt—
A married man is best "at home,"
　　And should be seldom "out."

Us Wisdom.

"WHEN Wisdom crieth in the street no man regardeth her ;" but when Wisdom goes into the House and gives Buchanan a pair of black eyes Wisdom is regarded a great deal, and has had to apologise.

Unreasonable Demands.

MR. BERRY complains that the people of Mordialloo are hard to satisfy. They have got a new school, they want a new gaol, and Mr. Berry says they will want a gallows next. True—and when they get it they'll be asking Melbourne to send them down some men to hang.

NOT much account when lecturing entertainments are concerned "The Judgment of Paris."

On 11 February 1884, the *Argus* reported: 'A marriage, in which more than ordinary interest has been manifested, took place on Saturday at Rupertswood, Sunbury, the residence of Sir William J. Clarke. The happy pair were the Hon. Ivo Francis Walter Bligh, second son of the Earl of Darnley, of Cobham Hall, Gravesend, Kent, England, and the popular captain of the last team of English cricketers which visited Australia, and Miss Florence Rose Morphy, youngest daughter of the late John Stephen Morphy, police magistrate, formerly of Beechworth. The ceremony was performed at St Mary's Church, Sunbury, by the Rev. W. C. Ford, the incumbent of the church, assisted by the Rev. H. N. Woollaston, of Trinity Church, East Melbourne. The church was tastefully festooned with flowers and heart-shaped wreaths intertwined. The choir was led by Mrs Ryan, and Lady Clarke, an intimate friend of the bride, was among the choristers.

'A special train arrived from Melbourne, conveying about 200 guests, who, on behalf of Mrs Morphy, had received invitations to be present.

'At half-past one, the bridal party entered the church, Miss Morphy leaning on the arm of Sir William Clarke, who gave her away. She was attired in a Princess brocaded white silk dress, trimmed with Honiton lace. The veil, of plain tulle, was fastened with a diamond arrow, the gift of the bridegroom. The bridesmaids, who wore Cambridge blue, were Miss Lily Snodgrass, Miss Lily Fisken, Miss Blanche Clarke, Miss Marion Jeffry, Miss Mary Clarke, Miss Baby Parkyns, Miss Jessie Osborne, and Miss Amy Parkins. Their baskets of flowers were of cerise and yellow, in compliment to the colours of the Bligh cricketing team. The groomsmen were Lord William Neville, Mr G. F. Vernon, Mr E. De Verdon, Mr A. F. Robinson, Mr Walter Clarke Warrington (private secretary to Sir William Des Voeux, Governor of Fiji), and Masters Clyde Clarke and Russell Clarke.

'The wedding breakfast took place in the new ballroom at Rupertswood, which was prettily decorated and inscribed. The dejeuner was rendered more enjoyable by the music of Plock's band.

'The bridegroom, in responding to the toast of the day, alluded in happy terms to the fact that he had, while captaining his team of cricketers, always found it easy to reply on their behalf after they had played a winning match, which he might be said to have done that morning.

'The toast list included the healths of Mrs Morphy, the parents of the bridegroom, Sir William and Lady Clarke, the clergy, and the Hon. Ivo Bligh's late comrades in the cricket field, on whose behalf Mr Vernon responded.

'The newly-wedded pair left early in the afternoon for the residence of Sir George Verdon, Macedon. Many of the guests remained to dance till ten o'clock in the evening. The special train left Sir William Clarke's private platform at half-past 10 pm and reached Melbourne three-quarters of an hour later.'

Beechworth's local weekly newspaper, the *Ovens and Murray Advertiser*, on 12 February, reported: 'The fashion event of the week has been the

Lady Janet Clarke—Copyright Michael Clarke   Sir William Clarke—Copyright Michael Clarke

marriage of the Honourable Ivo Bligh to Miss Florence Morphy, and as an evidence of the possibilities which the future holds in store for many a poor Australian maiden, it is quite romantic in the circumstances surrounding it. The lady possesses great personal attractions, which are enhanced by charming and loveable manners, which have constituted her quite a pet of society, and is the daughter of the late Mr John Stephen Morphy, a formerly warden of the Beechworth district. His death reduced his family to those straits of genteel poverty under which so many suffer; but they bore up bravely, and a Government appointment tendered to the widow somewhat helped them to fight the weary battle of life under the circumstances.

'The now newly-made bride, in whom Lady Clarke has for a long time past, evinced deep interest, met with her "fate" while travelling with her ladyship; and it is said that moonlight and the placid sea helped him wonderfully to the recognition of the charming lady who now stands so excellent a prospect of queening English society as Countess of Darnley.'

Ivo and Florence took up residence in East Melbourne and it was there in a modest little house called Hazelwell, in Powlett Street, that the first of the couple's three children, a boy whom they called Esme Ivo, was born in 1886.

109

Hazelwell, the house in Powlett Street, East Melbourne, where Ivo and Florence lived immediately after their marriage

The same year, in England, the Nottinghamshire and England fast bowler, Fred Morley, became increasingly ill and, despite having had the best medical attention over a period of eighteen months, he died in his home village of Sutton-in-Ashfield on 28 September, of lung congestion at the age of thirty-three. He had never fully recovered from his broken rib suffered in the collision of the *Peshawur* in the Indian Ocean. Home again, he had played in only one more match, against Lancashire, in 1883.

By 1888, Ivo and Florence had returned to England and a second son, Noel Gervase, was born in Palmyra Avenue, Brighton, Sussex.

On 10 May 1888, Reginald Brooks died in London. Twelve years later, on 5 October 1894, M. H. Spielmann wrote to a *Punch* magazine cartoonist, Linley Sambourne, seeking information about *Punch* writers for his history of the magazine.

The letter read: '. . . The Brooks matter is owing to the difficulties thrown in my way (the ones that I have met with, deliberately intended) by the Brooks' representatives. I'm surprised that I have got hold of as much as I have in respect of S.B. . . .'

On this letter is also (apparently) Sambourne's replies, written in red ink.

110

No. 6 Kent Terrace (left of centre), Baker Street, London—home of the Brooks family

These are: 'Who are the Brooks' representatives. R.S.B. died 1885 or 6. The other brother sank to a cab tout and was helped to Australia by a general subscription from the *Punch* Table.

'Shirley Brooks left an illegitimate son, I believe, by the name of Laidlaw and also a daughter, but I don't know what became of her. I heard of the son after S.B.'s death. Who has the S.B.'s papers etc. etc? I have a letter of S.B.'s, almost the last he ever wrote.'

Here, it seems, is more than enough reason to justify, in their day, the reluctance of Spielmann and Layard to let out the whole truth.

Reginald's final contribution to *Punch*, according to the contributors' ledger for 1880–85, was entitled 'Election Intelligence' and for this he was paid 15s 0d.

According to his death certificate, Reginald died on 10 May 1888, at 4 Bedford Place. The cause of death was 'pulmonary phthisis six months syncope' certified by John H. Vinrace MB. Attendant upon his death was William Farr Goldberg, of 52 Fleet Street.

Reginald was buried beside his parents in the rambling acres of Kensal Green Cemetery, North London.

111

The inscription on the family gravestone, under weeds and leaf mould in the shade of a London plane tree, reads:

Charles Shirley Brooks
died 23rd February 1874
aged 58 years
Emily Margaret
his wife
died 14th May 1880
aged 49 years
Reginald Shirley Walhinshaw
his eldest son
died 10th May, 1888
aged 34 years

Emily's birth certificate states 'Emily Marguerite'; that of Reginald, 'Reginald Shirley Watkinshaw.'

CHAPTER 10

The origins of Cobham Hall are obscured by mediaeval mists. When the Duke of Lennox and Richmond died in 1672, he left the Hall to his widow for the rest of her days. Then it passed to the Duke's sister, Lady Catherine O'Brien, who, on the death of her brother, had successfully claimed the barony of Clifton of Leighton Bromswold. By succession, the property eventually came to Lady Theodosia Hyde. In 1713, she married John Bligh,

Entrance to Cobham Hall, Kent, England

whose ancestors had settled in Ireland under Cromwell's rule.

The ambitious Mr Bligh was MP for Athboy. In 1721, he was created Baron Clifton of Rathmore, two years later, Viscount Darnley, and in 1725, the Earl of Darnley in the peerage of Ireland where he had estates of 10 000 acres. But John Bligh enjoyed his final elevation for only three years. He died in 1728 to be succeeded by his son, Edward, who had been Baron Clifton since the death of his mother in 1722.

For the next 100 years and more, the Cobham estates enjoyed expanding prosperity. This expansion came to a halt in 1835 with the death of the fifth Earl. The mantle was then taken up by John Stuart Bligh — Ivo's father — who had the longest reign of any Bligh at Cobham: Sixty-one years in which circumstances of tense pomp rode on the back of stagnation.

Rarely, observed one of the sixth Earl's contemporaries, could there have been a less happy man, or one less capable of inspiring happiness. Intensely repressed and inhibited, he probably never knew what it was like to take life easily and naturally. Blame for this may have rested with the Jesuit fathers responsible for his early education.

'Darnley,' as the new Earl insisted on being called, always lived by the 'rules.' He was a stickler for etiquette and punctuality was of paramount importance. Everyone subservient to him was haunted by the prospect of being an instant late in any task. Never at ease, the household was like an army permanently on parade with its commander.

Yet seldom was the Earl heard to raise his voice or lose his temper. He was an intensely shy man, always aware of the necessity to maintain his position in the splendour that was expected of him, and in the spirit of community service — a traditional quirk of the British aristocracy.

In 1850, Lord Darnley, to the astonishment of London society and the county set, forsook the family tradition of choosing an Irish bride and married Lady Harriet Mary Pelham, the eldest daughter of the third Earl of Chichester. This turned out to be an ideal match.

The new countess was tall as an Amazon and unbending as a stalagmite. She was as rigid and unresponsive as the Sphinx. 'How do you do,' she would murmur, extending limp fingers and, by this manner, terrified all youngsters who ventured near her.

Between the Earl and the Countess, there were subtle differences, however, but opportunity to observe these fell only to the few in their tight little inner circle of acquaintances. In fact, the Earl had a vivid personality which gave rise to many stories; his wife, on the other hand, had a presence capable of making plunge a temperature already at zero. The confidences of husband and wife were never broken. Perhaps they hatched a conspiracy of silence.

Every morning for years, whatever the weather in the open air outside his bedroom, Lord Darnley shaved there and read his Bible.

He was particularly rigid about the smoking of tobacco. This indulgence was strictly for men, then only in a special room — and jackets, used only for this purpose, were compulsory.

Stored in the smoking room was a box of deluxe cigars. Lord Darnley allowed only himself to touch that box and dispense its contents to particularly honoured guests. That box could not be breathed on, not even by a maid with a feather duster.

Now Lord Darnley had a favourite son — not Ivo, but Arthur, his third boy. One night, the male guests ambled to the smoking room and settled down to await the Earl's arrival. Something must have delayed the old man and Arthur, stirred by the impatience of youth, began offering the hallowed box round the company.

'Arthur, *what* are you going?' came a soft voice, charged with thunder. Lord Darnley had quietly entered.

'Merely your duty as a host, father,' replied his favourite, only pausing for a moment in his task.

This left Lord Darnley dumbfounded and the company pondering on whether anyone else in the household could have carried off such a manner.

While the Earl's tongue was quiet, his pen knew no such inhibition. Lord Darnley was an enthusiastic writer of letters to editors; he had also a talent for verse.

Out of doors he was addicted to shooting, but abominated the chase. Consequently, he was never short of a theme for letters.

This John Darnley died in 1896, thus ending abruptly the Victorian splendour of Cobham. His eldest son, Edward Bligh, inherited the earldom. For the servants, the eternal parade might be over, but much worse was in store.

The seventh Earl was a giant, a tearaway with a fearsome temper and a fire-cracker mind on a short fuse. His hand at the Cobham helm was as catastrophic as a cloud bursting over a one-day cricket match.

In short, he raped the place. Mercifully, the nightmare lasted for only four years. When he died in 1900, he was survived by an only child, a daughter only a few months old whom he had endowed bountifully with, among many other items of great value, priceless china and tapestries collected at Cobham by his grandfather. The endowment became a significant factor as an aggravation in the continuing decline of the seat.

Ivo, then, unexpectedly found himself the master of a virtually ravaged home which had been the victim, twice in rapid succession, of savage new death duties designed to hit the great estates, and of the rampages of his brother, Edward.

A contemporary recalled Ivo saying that he estimated the drop of Cobham's agricultural rents in the last part of the century as something not less than fifty per cent, but added that this had been to a considerable extent compensated for by the effects of the expansion of Rochester in converting an increasing margin of impoverished agricultural land to richly-paying urban building sites.

The estate, the eighth Earl quickly discovered, could remain intact only by the progressive sacrifice of what chanced to still survive in the building.

But of the Victorian Earl's brood of eight, Ivo, at least, knew how to enjoy life—something which had always seemed to be denied his father. For the first time in the living memory of most people at Cobham, everyone was able to relax.

Despite his crippling financial inheritance, Ivo, taking advantage of the characteristics once so abundantly evident in him as a cricket captain, refused to accept defeat. Supported by his happy family, he seemed to bring Australia's sunshine to Cobham.

One of Ivo's most treasured experiences while master of Cobham Hall must surely have been in arranging a cricket match between a Cobham Village team and a team of Australians led by General Sir William Birdwood who commanded the Australian and New Zealand Army Corps at Gallipoli and later became Lord Birdwood.

By their very nature, sequels are neat, wholesome, and consequently offer a source of satisfaction. There is no evidence to suggest that either participants or observers of this match played at Cobham during the summer of 1919 saw it as a sequel to that played on the cricket paddock at Rupertswood almost forty years earlier, but the circumstances of each are too comfortably similar to escape some significance now.

The few Australians who previously knew of this encounter have very good reason to try to forget about it. Cobham scored 106 and the Australians replied with a total of 36, being shattered by C. Daniels who claimed all ten of the visitors' wickets. The original details of this encounter were probably lost in a pavilion fire at the ground some years later.

Of course, cricket had been played at Cobham since mediaeval days when shepherd boys probably wielded their crooks and convenient meadow gates were used as stumps. The ball was perhaps a bundle of wool. Crude cricket, indeed, but satisfying and sufficiently enjoyable to endure and evolve into the fascinating game which Ivo and the others, who went in pursuit of the Ashes, kept alive so vigorously.

One of the earliest recorded games at Cobham was in 1776. Mr Richard Hayes, of Owletts, Cobham, wrote in his diary for 26 June: 'To see Cobham play Addington. Played one hands apiece only, so they agreed not to play tomorrow, Cobham had rather ye worse of it, although they beat Addington much when they played there.'

There are also records of Kent having played Hampshire at Cobham in 1791, but it was not until 1850 that the ground was put in order and cricket played there regularly.

On 7 August 1850, twenty-two players sporting top hats and mostly wearing whiskers met in Cobham Park where the wickets were pitched for a game to mark the birth of Cobham Cricket Club. This match between the Hall and the Village was the first of many such encounters.

It appears from the records that the standard of play from 1853 was very high. Cobham's opponents in those years were such sides as Gravesend, Rochester, Dartford, and Malling. Cobham usually won.

116

Ivo's father always footed the bill for the maintenance of the ground. It was soon known as one of the finest, best-equipped grounds in the country and existed for the enjoyment of anyone who could reach Cobham Park.

The developing club produced some of England's finest cricketers and perhaps the earliest of these was George Bennett.

The Darnley Arms in Cobham, Kent, England

117

Bennett was born at Shorne in 1829 and worked as a bricklayer at Cobham Hall. He played regularly for Kent and was a member of the team which visited Australia in 1862 under the leadership of H. H. Stephenson. He was also for ten years the professional at Eton. His best performance was in a North versus South match at Lord's in 1865 when he scored 100 against the finest bowling of the day. George Collins, a bowler, was another Cobham man who played for Kent for many years.

In May 1925, most of Lord Darnley's collection of pictures by English and foreign old masters were sold at Christie's. There were ninety-one lots and these made the then surprising total of £70758. Seven pictures made four-figure sums, including Hoppner's portrait of Lady Elizabeth Bligh (10200 guineas) and of the fourth Earl of Darnley (3100 guineas). Sir Joshua Reynolds's 'The Calling of Samuel' made 6700 guineas, Gainsborough's portrait of Mrs W. Mouk, 4800 guineas, and Sir Antonio Mor's 'Portrait of a Lady', 4200 guineas.

Early on the morning of Palm Sunday, 10 April 1927, at Puckle Hill House, Shorne, Ivo Francis Walter Bligh, the eighth Earl of Darnley, had a fatal heart attack. He was found by his valet. There had been no warning. The previous afternoon, the Earl had enjoyed a round of golf. He was sixty-eight.

The county flag at Rochester Castle was flown at half-mast and the great bell in the cathedral was tolled.

The Times recorded: '. . . Lord Darnley was very tall and of slender build, but he made full use of his height and had very strong wrists, was as fine a cutter of the ball as any of his contemporaries, and was a good hitter all round the wicket. He had one fault, and that was that his defence was marred by a crooked bat, but he had so good an eye that he was not as handicapped as might have been expected . . . He was elected a representative peer for Ireland in 1905, and was Deputy Lieutenant and County Alderman for Kent . . .'

The *Gravesend Reporter* said: 'He took an active share in the public life of the district and was a great benefactor. He was president of the Cobham Village Club, and to him that social centre owes its very existence. He was chairman of the parish council; vicar's warden till 1925; and president of the Cobham Cricket Club . . .

'Many local charities and benefit associations had his Lordship's support and he was interested in agricultural and business organisations. A few years ago, he presided at a League of Nations meeting in Chatham Town Hall and spoke on disarmament. He was a prominent figure at Conservative gatherings and was constant in his support of the party. He was president of the Kent Constitutional Association . . . When Lord Darnley was at Eton, he was one of the two boy editors of the school magazine, *The Eton Chronicle*. Referring to these editorial experiences in a speech last year (1926) to the students of Gravesend County School for Boys at their prize day, he said: "During my editorship, Mr Gladstone, himself an old Etonian, made a speech to the Marlborough boys which we thought was disparaging to his old school, so we employed our best leading-article writer to write an article giving the great man snuff. So successful was the article that Mr Gladstone wrote me an autograph letter, explaining away the speech in his own inimitable style, and I still have the letter at Cobham . . ."'

CHAPTER 11

The life of the eighth Countess of Darnley offers perhaps as much mystery as the Ashes themselves. In *The Complete Peerage* in 1916, the Hon. Vicary Gibbs claimed: 'She was a niece of Morphy, the celebrated chess-player.' Mr Gibbs (1853–1932) was born at Hampstead and educated at Eton and Christ Church, Oxford. He became a genealogist and gardener.

The father of Florence, John Stephen Morphy, was born in 1812. According to the *Gravesend Reporter*, he came from a well-known Irish family of Killarney, of royal descent, and one of the oldest in Kerry.

But 'Morphy, the celebrated chess-player' was an American, born in New Orleans in 1837, who became the Bobby Fischer of his day. He died in 1884, aged forty-seven, his mother finding him dead in a bath. Paul Morphy had only one brother, born on 26 December 1834, and called Edward. The chess genius also had two sisters: Mahrina, born on 5 February 1830, and Helena born on 21 October 1839.

Florence was born on 25 August 1860, and was not quite eleven months old when her father died on 13 July 1861. She had been baptised Rose Florence Morphy on 5 April that year in Beechworth by the Rev. W. Corbet Howard.

Mrs Morphy, left with a family of seven, was thus reduced to what came to be described as 'genteel poverty'. She was given 'a Government appointment' and had an income of rent from family property in Beechworth. Such were the circumstances from which Florence continued in anonymity—until Ivo appeared on the scene some twenty years later.

Ivo returned to England by 1888, but when did he first take his wife to Cobham Hall—while his father, the sixth Earl, was still alive? If this happened, one wonders what sort of a reception was accorded to Florence? Did her charisma have the effect on them that it seemed to have on everybody else she met, both in Australia and England, throughout her long and extraordinary life? Did the iceberg of an old Earl and his stalagmite wife see in their daughter-in-law a fortune hunter, or recognise in her the most valuable acquisition to the Blighs in the long history of that family?

Florence, when she became the new Countess in 1900, was eager to promote anything associated with arts and crafts—she also became deeply involved in community welfare. It was her enthusiasm which led to the popularity of local lacemaking. Classes for this were formed in fourteen villages around Cobham. Florence became an intimate of Queen Mary and lace handkerchiefs were once presented to the Queen and to the Princess Royal.

Sailing on the P. & O. liner *Ophir*, Florence visited Australia in 1904, accompanied by her third and last child, Lady Dorothy. At Beechworth, the Countess presented the Anglican Christ Church with an autographed *Book of Common Prayer*.

Florence, Countess of Darnley

121

Father Malcolm Crawley, of Christ Church, Beechworth, with the prayer book which was presented to the church by the Countess of Darnley

Cobham Hall was used as a military hospital for five years from October 1914, and more than 2000 Australians passed through it. Florence acted as the matron. Over Christmas 1917, the Australian Prime Minister, Mr W. M. Hughes, visited the men at Cobham. Among these were some young and ambitious airmen. During the Christmas dinner, according to the *Gravesend Reporter*, some of the airmen approached the Countess and asked her to try to persuade Mr Hughes to agree to them having the privilege of making the first attempt to fly from England to Australia. She did this and the Prime Minister agreed to do what he could.

Two years later, with Ross Smith at its controls, a Vickers Vimy bomber clattered into the skies over southern England and into aviation history.

A memorial inscription at Adelaide Airport reads: 'On November 12, 1919, two South Australians, Captain Ross Smith MC DFC AFC, and Lieutenant Keith Smith, set out from Hounslow, near London, for Australia in a Vickers Vimy long-range bomber. With them were two Australian air mechanics, Sergeant J. M. Bennett AFM MSM and Sergeant W. H. Sheers MSM.

'Twenty-seven days later, on December 10, 1919, having flown 11 060 miles through France, Italy, Crete, Egypt, Palestine, Mesopotamia, Persia, India, Burma, Siam, Malaya and the Dutch East Indies, they landed at Darwin to win a £10 000 prize offered by the Commonwealth Government for the first Australians to fly from England to Australia in less than 30 days.

'Their flight won them a proud place among the pioneers of civil aviation. On December 22, their remarkable feat received its highest recognition when Captain Ross Smith and Lieutenant Keith Smith were knighted by His Majesty King George V.'

Ross described the aircraft's landing at Darwin as 'the supreme moment of our lives'. Telegrams and cables awaiting them seemed to be from everyone everywhere—King George V: 'Delighted at your safe arrival . . .' The British Prime Minister, Mr Lloyd George: '. . . Your flight shows how the inventions of war can advance the progress of peace.' And Mr Hughes: '. . . They are Empire builders . . . They have added fresh laurels to the name of Australia . . .'

In 1919, Florence was made a Dame of the British Empire. Her many public offices included the presidency of the Linen League at St Bartholomew's Hospital, Rochester. She was also president of the Girls' Home in Chatham; of the Gravesend branch of the National Society for the Prevention of Cruelty to Children; the Gravesend Girl Guides; the Gravesend Habit of the Primrose League; the Rochester and West Kent Art Society; and the Cobham and Luddesdowne Nursing Association.

Not long before Ivo's death, the Darnley family home was transferred from Cobham Hall to nearby Puckle Hill House in Shorne Woods. The house overlooks Cobham Park and the Countess, who took a keen interest in horticulture, transformed her new environment by creating terraced gardens. Her ability as a water diviner was useful in this project.

Belatedly, the Countess took up painting and successfully captured the cascading colour of Cobham Woods in the rhododendron season. Also on travels, she worked on many landscapes of Inverness, Sutherland, Devon and France. Many of these pictures were sold to aid charity.

Florence was also able to express herself in music and prose. She wrote the song Content, several hymns and the waltzes Southern Cross and Bonheur. The latter was composed for the coming-out of her daughter, Lady Dorothy.

Florence also wrote short stories for magazines, and, in collaboration with

123

a friend, a novel entitled *Elma Trevor*. Such achievements suggest her well capable of penning the verse attached to the Ashes urn, but which lacks any credit.

Florence, the Dowager Countess of Darnley, left Puckle Hill House in the early days of the second World War and, as Londoners gritted their teeth against waves of flying bombs, she died on Wednesday, 30 August 1944, at Bellehatch Park, Henley-on-Thames, the home of Lady Rathcreden.

The *Gravesend Reporter*, in its obituary, said: '. . . Thus passes a noble, clever and extremely versatile woman — one who by her grace and charm won a high place in the estimation and affection of all . . .'

In *The Times*, Field Marshall Lord Birdwood wrote: 'I know full well that I am voicing the feelings of a vast number of my old Australian comrades in attempting to pay tribute to the memory of Florence, Lady Darnley. During the 1914–18 war, large numbers of Australian sick and wounded came over here and the Darnleys converted their lovely old Kentish home — Cobham Hall — into an Australian hospital. I know personally how fully and deeply those men appreciated all that was done for them, and especially because they realised they owed everything to the unsparing devotion of their host and hostess. Lady Darnley never ceased in her energies to see that the patients wanted for nothing, and many a home in Australia today will be deeply regretting the passing away of one whom they know never forgot them, while the many friends she leaves behind, who knew and loved her, will never cease to mourne her loss.'

The *Reporter* also added: 'The romantic story of her wedding, which was supposed to have originated by the meeting of her future husband (the late Earl), on the cricket ground at Melbourne, is known the world over. Unfortunately, it lacked the merit of being strictly true. Actually she was introduced to Lord Darnley (then the Hon. Ivo Bligh) at a dinner at the residence of Sir William and Lady Clarke the night after his arrival from England. Lord Darnley had his arm in a sling — he had hurt it during a tug of war on the boat and was thus unable to play in the opening match. Subsequently at Melbourne, he cut his finger while fielding the ball and his bride-to-be bound it up for him in the pavilion. It was Sir William Clarke who presented Lord Darnley with the famous urn of ashes . . .'

CHAPTER 12

William John Clarke, the eldest of the three sons of 'Big' Clarke and his wife, Eliza, was born on 31 March 1831, at Lovely Banks, Van Diemen's Land, (now Tasmania). His parents had emigrated from Bridgewater in Somerset.

Young William was educated first at Bonwick's Academy in Hobart, then in England at Whitchurch Grammar School, Shropshire. He returned home in 1850 and spent some years learning to manage his father's expanding properties in Victoria.

Eventually, with his younger brother, Joseph, he went to manage the family estates in Tasmania and they lived at Norton Mandeville. William became a member of the Hamilton Road Board and a Justice of the Peace. On 23 August 1860, he married Mary Walker and the couple went to live at Sunbury in Victoria.

William and Mary had two sons and two daughters. The eldest child, Rupert, was born in 1865.

Mary died on 14 April 1871. Almost two years later, on 21 January 1873, William married Janet Snodgrass. The next year, William's father died, leaving him all the Victorian properties. These were then worth about £1 500 000. Thus William became the biggest landowner in the colony.

He began building the mansion, Rupertswood, and lavish spending became the style for the remainder of his life. He travelled widely and became a leader of colonial society.

He was keen about scientific farming and was on the committee of several Victorian horticultural societies. He imported farm machinery and introduced Leicester sheep to Australia.

Dowling Forest, near Ballarat, he turned into a model farming estate. A Shorthorn stud was established at Bolinda Vale and he brought in Aberdeen Angus cattle when they were still a rarity. He bought property in Queensland.

William also bred horses and his filly, Petrea, won the Victorian Oaks in 1879. His yacht, Janet, won the first intercolonial yacht race in 1881. From 1880 to 1886, he was the president of the Melbourne Cricket Club. Many charities benefited from his support.

In 1882, he and his wife visited England and established the 3000-guineas Clarke music scholarship at the Royal College of Music. The baronetcy, on his return to Australia, was in recognition of his services as president of the Melbourne Exhibition of 1880–81.

William also inherited his father's big share in the Colonial Bank of Australia and he served as its governor for twenty years.

Like other banks, it became involved in speculation and William lost heavily in the 1893 crash. The bank recovered, however, mainly because William came to the rescue with his own capital. But the pressures involved took their toll and he died suddenly, of a heart attack, on 15 May 1897. His

The Hon. Michael Clarke—Copyright the *Age* newspaper

estate was divided between his widow and ten surviving children.

His instinctive generosity won the observation that 'he revels in benevolence, and derives the greater part of his own happiness from his unfailing efforts to render others happy.'

Apart from his sharply-contrasting happy disposition, William, in many ways, can be seen as the Australian counterpart of the sixth Earl of Darnley, doing for the State of Victoria what Lord Darnley did for Cobham and Kent.

At Rupertswood, then, Ivo probably felt at home and perhaps discovered himself able to relax more there than in his tense youth at regimented Cobham.

How Rupertswood became associated with the Ashes is explained by the Hon. Michael Clarke, a grandson of Sir William, who lives in Victoria. He was born at Rupertswood and educated at Harrow and New College, Oxford. He is a solicitor, farmer, author, and a former State MP.

Mr Clarke says that diaries to which the Clarke family has access reveal that Ivo Bligh and his cricketers were visitors at Rupertswood on 25 27 November and at Christmas 1882, and on New Year's Day and 20–22 January 1883.

The story of the Ashes was told to Mr Clarke when he was a boy by Pat Lyons, an ancient bearded character who chopped firewood at Rupertswood, had worked for 'Big' Clarke, been the dairyman at Rupertswood in 1882–83 and was a great raconteur of past events.

Pat Lyons, who had played cricket himself on the Rupertswood ground, told Mr Clarke that the English cricketers played a social game with other gentlemen on the cricket paddock, a sloping piece of land between the house and the railway line. This was about Christmas time. There was some mighty hitting, and the servants were kept busy retrieving the ball after 4s and 6s.

Pat Lyons, according to Mr Clarke, said: 'They knocked the cover off the ball, and afterwards it was burnt and the ashes put in a vase or something and given to the English captain, who married Florrie Morphy from Sunbury the following year. He was a lord and he took those ashes to England.'

On Christmas Day, 1882, says Mr Clarke, there was a dinner and dance in the ballroom and iron, gold and steel mementoes were given to the Englishmen by Lady Clarke as souvenirs of the *Peshawur*.

Mr Clarke says: 'My father, Russell Clarke, and my uncle, Sir Frank Clarke, used to argue whether the bails or ball were burnt. Local tradition favoured the ball, but my uncle had doubts as to whether one could burn a cricket ball. They agreed that it was not the stumps — which were borrowed from the local cricket club; and they thought that the bails would also be borrowed.

'I don't know for certain whether the Rupertswood ashes are The Ashes or not, but my father and uncle were convinced they were, and expressed scorn of other stories about their origin.

'I gathered that the cricket historians were reluctant to accept a version based upon a social game at Rupertswood, and preferred one based upon a Test match or other grand occasion.

'I well remember visiting the then Lord Darnley at Cobham in England when I was a schoolboy (about 1933). He showed my mother and I over the house and remarked that both his mother and the cricket Ashes came from Sunbury.'

Mr Clarke has, in his possession, a black bail. This serves as the handle of an ivory paperknife. On the blade of the paperknife is an inscription: 'England v Australia, January 26, 1883. England won by 69 runs. This bail was knocked off by the last ball bowled in the match.' Engraved below this

127

are the initials J.M.C.—presumably Janet Marion Clarke.

Another memento of 1882–83, privately owned in Melbourne, is a silver salver which was presented to Lady Janet as a reciprocal gift from Ivo Bligh's team. The salver is inscribed with their names.

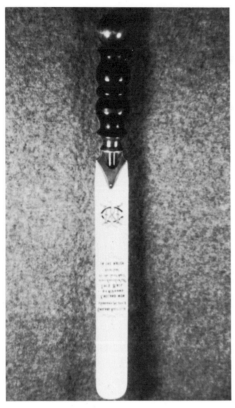

One of the bails believed to have escaped the flames. It now serves as the handle of an ivory paperknife. Copyright Michael Clarke

Inscription on the paperknife. Copyright Michael Clarke.

CHAPTER 13

The Marylebone Cricket Club is indebted, for its origins, to a bustling Yorkshireman. Thomas Lord was drawn to London from Thirsk. He became a prosperous wine merchant and formed associations with the nobility which led to his involvement in the aristocratic White Conduit Club.

Lord made a very favourable impression here and the members began urging him to open his own cricket ground. He did this, taking over land at Dorset Fields in 1787 and calling it the Marylebone Cricket Club. It was immediately a popular place for the wealthy who were able to devote their time to cricket. Its popularity, however, could not prevent financial problems.

The landowners demanded more rent, so Lord leased another ground at North Bank, Regent's Park. But attitudes changed with the venue and this never enjoyed the popularity of the first site. Within a few years, the Regent's Canal was cut through the playing area. Lord was not unduly discouraged. He moved the club to another home—land in St John's Wood which gradually became recognised as the MCC's permanent home, an integral part of the Establishment, and the power centre of the cricket world.

Today, the freehold of Lord's is owned by the MCC. The club leases the ground to the Middlesex Cricket Club, and cricket's other chief administrative bodies, the Test and County Cricket Board and the International Cricket Council, are cloistered here. The MCC administers Lord's and currently has the patronage of the Queen.

Also within the precincts of Lord's is the Memorial Gallery. Formerly a rackets court, this was opened in 1953 by H.R.H. Prince Philip—president of the MCC in 1949—as a memorial to all the cricketers who lost their lives in the second World War. Among the collected relics on display here is the urn reputedly still containing the Ashes . . .

To handle the Ashes urn would be easy enough, but its guardians, the MCC, claim that no one is allowed to tamper with it for fear of damage. It is, for many, the most treasured reminder of cricket past, and irreplaceable— perhaps.

According to an MCC catalogue, the urn is of dark red pottery, presumably Australian, and contains the ashes of a bail sealed by a cork.

The urn is 10·6 cm tall, with the cork 10·8 cm, and has a base 3·5 cm in diameter. The width of the shoulder is approximately 4·1 cm. The urn has two handles and these taper downwards to a moulded stem and base.

Attached to the body of the urn are two labels. One is inscribed 'The Ashes' and on the other is a verse: this reads:

> *When Ivo goes back with the urn, the urn;*
> *Studds, Steel, Read and Tylecote return, return;*
> *The welkin will ring loud,*

The great crowd will feel proud,
Seeing Barlow and Bates with the urn, the urn;
And the rest coming home with the urn.

Not attributed to anybody, the verse is probably the piece of Australian literature, if it is Australian, most consistently in the public gaze and given the least consideration.

The verse immediately prompts questions: When did Ivo take home the urn? Did the great crowd ever see Barlow, Bates, and the rest with the urn? Who wrote the verse?

While Ivo doubtlessly returned to England as the hero of English cricketing circles—he was reputedly canonised by *Punch* magazine—what sort of reception was waiting for him at home, at Cobham Hall in Kent?

Could it be that he discovered himself the black sheep of the family? Since setting out for Australia the previous September, he had met on a ship, and now intended to marry, a virtually penniless Australian servant girl.

What was the reaction to this news of his father, the sixth Earl of Darnley, who had once appealed to his fellow Peers in the House of Lords for recognition in the ranks of royalty—and had been rejected? Some of the servants at Cobham Hall were probably better off financially than Florence Morphy. Ivo sailed again for Australia late in 1883—with or without his father's blessing?

Meanwhile, where was the urn? If Ivo's reception at Cobham was less than fond, perhaps he would have expected it and not taken the urn along. To hold it aloft triumphantly on his arrival might have been rather like showing a red rag to a bull. Least likely of all, surely, is the possibility that he left the urn at Cobham when he returned to Australia. His father might well have hurled it through the nearest window. So the safest place to have left the urn would probably have been with his beloved Florence, waiting in Melbourne. As well as a symbol of cricketing glory, it would also have served as a token of his faith.

If the urn was left with Florence, then the Ashes did not reach England before 1886 (when Esme was born in Melbourne) and probably not until 1888 (when Noel was born in Brighton).

There is no date with the verse, but it carries the implication of being written while Bligh was on the tour:

'When Ivo goes back with the urn, the urn . . .'

Its composition was obviously well within the capability of Florence, but there were others around, in both Melbourne and Sydney, who were equally able—Lady Janet Clarke, and her sister, Lily Snodgrass, and Blanche Clarke.

On the other hand, the verse could well have been written much later, perhaps even in England, to support the popular story of the 'recovery' of the Ashes in 1883 which has become legend.

Many authorities, including the late Lord Gowrie, have stressed that the

130

urn was Bligh's private property, yet the verse implies that it was meant for the whole team. The present Lady Clarke goes along with this, believing it likely that Lady Janet organised the burning of the Ashes perhaps at the instigation of young Russell Clarke.

For more than thirty years, Australians have unwittingly entertained a false impression concerning a replica of the romantic Ashes urn. They have believed, with good reason, that the replica, a gift from Marylebone Cricket Club at Lord's and currently displayed in Sydney, is unique. This is not so, and never was.

The false impression was first given in 1948 by the then President of the MCC, Lord Gowrie, who was a war hero, Privy Councillor, and a former Governor General of Australia.

It was 29 October 1948, that Lord Gowrie wrote to the chairman of the Australian Cricket Board of Control: 'The term "Ashes" is derived from a small pottery urn presented to the Hon. Ivo Bligh in 1883 in Melbourne. This urn, as is explained in the enclosed historic note, was, of course, his private property and after his death was presented to the MCC.

'It has occurred to the MCC that many people in Australia would like to have the opportunity of seeing this, and we have accordingly had an exact facsimile made which is being sent separately as a gift from us to the Australian Board of Control.

'You will understand that this is probably our most prized possession in the collected of cricket relics and naturally we do not propose to have other copies made.'

This last sentence of Lord Gowrie's, however, contradicts the MCC minutes dated 12 April 1948—a good six months before Lord Gowrie's letter was written.

The minutes record: 'The secretary was instructed to have three replicas made and of these, it was agreed that one should be offered to the Australian Board of Control at the end of the 1948 season . . .'

The MCC secretary at that time was Colonel R. S. Rait Kerr and the museum curator was his daughter, Miss Diana Rait Kerr. When the discrepancy was pointed out, Miss Rait Kerr said: '. . . My only comment would be that, although Lord Gowrie was mistaken, I am quite certain that he wrote in good faith.'

But Lord Gowrie's tone was emphatic: '. . . and naturally we do not propose to have other copies made.' It suggests that he would have opposed any such proposal.

The questions prompted immediately are: How did Lord Gowrie come to make such an error? Did he write the letter himself—or merely put his signature to it?

Perhaps the late Colonel Rait Kerr wrote the letter, but the instructions to have the replicas made were given to him; and he was once described by the late Sir Pelham Warner (another MCC man) as 'the ablest secretary the MCC ever possessed . . .'

131

The condition of the replica urn in Sydney, incidently, has always worried the Australian Cricket Board officials. It was damaged in transit from England and does not often leave Sydney.

Unhappy with its own plaster-of-paris replicas, the MCC has more recently had made some virtually unbreakable fibreglass replicas. These are occasionally loaned to promote good causes.

In June 1978, in a contribution to the *Sunday Times*, of London, it was suggested that the contents of the urn might well be blowing in the wind. Characteristically, the MCC neither confirmed nor denied this . . .

The urn currently on display at Lord's is alleged to be the original, yet how can we be sure? The viewing public, separated from the object as always by a glass panel, would be unable to tell the difference between the original and a replica.

But perhaps this is possible without the necessity of great expertise. The MCC offers for sale a colour postcard of the urn. There is also inside the back cover of an MCC souvenir booklet a black and white photograph of the urn taken in 1976 by the renowned cricket photographer, Mr Patrick Eagar, and the more recently taken of the two.

When compared, both photographs reveal that the cork in the urn is chipped. On Mr Eagar's picture (which he is confident is of the original urn), the chip is on the right-hand side of the urn, but in the colour picture the chip is shown quite clearly to be on the left.

What conclusions can be reached from this observation? There is a range of possibilities. If both pictures are, indeed, of the original urn, then in the interval between the taking of them, the cork was either removed, or an attempt was made to remove it. As the cork was turned through not fewer than 180 degrees, it would have seemed a simple task to take it out completely; and whoever did that would then be able to answer the most vital question. But the MCC officials maintain that the urn, owing to its extreme fragility, is never tampered with, implying by this that the cork has never been taken out in their experience, nor likely to be.

If there are Ashes still in the urn, then analysis by modern technology could surely determine them to be of a bail, stump, bat, or ball. Authorities at various times have suggested all these. It is perhaps the consequences of such determination which prevents the MCC having this done — unless it has already been done?

If one of the pictures is of a replica, then, having no reason to doubt Mr Eagar's word, the colour picture must be of it — and a poor replica at that by virtue of the chipped cork on the wrong side.

The remaining possibility is that both pictures are of replica urns . . .

The urn, in its display case on the left flank of stairs leading to the upper floor of the gallery, is not alone. Beside it is the velvet bag, a letter written by Ivo Bligh, and an embroidery design.

The explanatory notice says: '. . . The velvet bag was the gift of Mrs J. W. Fletcher of Brisbane. The embroidery design, and the Hon. Ivo Bligh's letter

Young Mrs Ann Fletcher

The elderly Mrs Ann Fletcher

thanking her, were the gift of Mrs Fletcher's daughter, Mrs M. D. McLaurin, in 1957.' Who was Mrs Fletcher?

Mrs Fletcher began life as Ann Clarke—and, as far as is known, had no association with the Clarkes of Melbourne. Usually called Annie, she was the daughter of Joseph Hines Clarke and Marion Clarke (nee Wright), of Dublin, Ireland.

Joseph Clarke was a member of the Royal Irish Regiment and, with the rank of 2nd Lieutenant, he fought in the Maori wars in New Zealand from about 1863–66. He is believed to have retired from the army with the rank of captain or major and travelled to Australia where he became interested in geology.

Ann came to Australia with her parents, but her only brother is thought to have stayed in New Zealand. In 1876, Ann married John Walter Fletcher at the Anglican Church of St Thomas, North Sydney.

John Fletcher was probably born in or near Redhill, Surrey. Certainly he went to school in Redhill. His first school exercise book still survives. Later, he went to Cheltenham Grammar School, and then to Pembroke College, Oxford.

John Fletcher was an outstanding sportsman. Trophies won during his university days are still in the possession of his grandchildren. He won his Blue at Oxford for long-distance running. He excelled at most games and athletics, and it is said that he and a Mr Southey played the first game of lawn tennis in Australia. He was also one of the instigators of soccer and golf in Australia.

Ann helped John in all his endeavours, contributing courage and cheerfulness in adversity. After managing a school successfully in Sydney, they moved to Katoomba in the Blue Mountains with the intention of starting another school, but this project did not work out as they hoped. The bank collapse in 1893 meant that many people could no longer afford to send their sons to such establishments. The Fletchers were forced to return to Sydney where Ann ran a boarding house while John studied law.

He was called to the Bar of New South Wales in 1892, and from 1900 till his retirement in 1915, travelled to all parts of NSW as a relief police magistrate. He died in a private hospital at Neutral Bay on 17 March 1918, after a long illness.

Ann and John had six children—Grace, Nora, Dorothy, John William, Judith, and Eric. It was Dorothy who became Mrs M. D. McLaurin. She loved literature and history, and wrote the life of Sir Henry Parkes which was published about twenty-five years ago. Dorothy married a Scottish electrical engineer.

Ann's seven surviving grandchildren have memories of her long skirts and her cheerfulness, despite a hacking cough during her later years.

In Sydney, Ann's eldest son, John William Fletcher, played cricket in the Paddington team with Victor Trumper and Montague Noble. He is mentioned in Jack Fingleton's book, *Victor Trumper.* John moved by chance to Queensland

135

Ann Fletcher and cat with (from left) Dorothy, Eric, and Nora. Front row, from left: Judith and Grace

and played cricket for that State in 1909–10. He became known in many fields before his death in 1965.

Ann Fletcher was a much-gifted woman and perhaps her greatest enjoyment was in needlework. She and her husband lived in various parts of Sydney — Elizabeth Bay, Paddington, and Woollahra. Ann spent the autumn of her years at Greenwich Point and it was here that she died in her eighty-fifth year in 1935 or 1936.

One of Ann Fletcher's grandchildren, Miss Joan M. Fletcher, believes that the velvet bag was perhaps presented to Ivo Bligh by Lady Carrington on behalf of Mrs Fletcher who was unable to take part in the festivities associated with the touring cricketers. Lady Carrington's husband became the Governor of New South Wales from 1885–90.

Recognising that the urn was a much more appropriate resting place for the Ashes than the velvet bag, Miss Fletcher wonders if, in fact, the urn was presented to Bligh at a later time than the bag. She thinks it unlikely that the bag would have been made and presented, had the existence of the urn been known.

Miss Fletcher believes that originally the Ashes were perhaps put in any old tin or container that happened to be convenient at the time of the burning and that the bag was meant as a more suitable container for the memento to travel to England.

The bag was probably made to contain the old tin, says Miss Fletcher. Ash would need to be in something inside a bag . . .

The letter displayed with the urn and the bag at Lord's is a note of thanks from Ivo Bligh to Mrs Fletcher. On 'Australian Club' notepaper, and dated 'Friday morning', it reads:

'My dear Mrs Fletcher, Many thanks for the pretty little bag you have so kindly sent me. The ashes shall be consigned to it forthwith and always kept there in memory of the great match. I shall be very pleased to accept Mrs Mann's invitation for Sunday. As far as I can ascertain at present, I shall be the only member . . .'

At this point, the notepaper is folded. Approached regarding the text of the other side, the Lord's museum curator, Mr Stephen Green, said: 'Ivo Bligh's letter was to thank Mrs. Fletcher for her gift of the velvet bag. I regret I cannot easily remove it from its present display panel, but I know from our catalogue that this was the gist of the letter.'

Referring to the letter, Miss Fletcher says that Bligh appeared to put no significance on their (the Ashes) container, but did value the ashes as symbolical instead of the previously only mythical ones of English cricket it was said he had come to recover.

'In those days,' continues Miss Fletcher, 'it was probably considered unbecoming behaviour for a married woman, except through the agency of another, to send a present to a gentleman. Perhaps it was done by a messenger who waited for a covering note from Lady Carrington and was then sent on to the club where he again waited. Bligh certainly seems to have only just received the bag and the invitation. Lack of telephones is the only explanation I can offer for the circuitous way the invitation was accepted. One Mrs. Mann was an aunt (of mine), the daughters of another were my grand-mother's life-long friends.'

Miss Fletcher believes that the theory that the Ashes were originally presented in the urn makes nonsense of the letter—rather that it supports her 'old tin' belief.

In the letter, Bligh refers to the ashes as being 'in memory of the great match'. *Wisden*, in reporting the fourth and final Test, referred to 'the great match of the tour'.

The design for the bag also offers scope for some speculation. Apparently the painter, William Blamire Young, was a friend of the family. He often did designs for Ann Fletcher's embroidery.

Young was a Yorkshireman—from Londesborough. Born in 1862, he was educated at Walthamstow Forest School and at Pembroke College, Cambridge. He taught himself art and was painting in watercolours before he was appointed assistant master at Katoomba College—run by John and Ann

137

Fletcher—in the Blue Mountains of New South Wales in 1885. During this period, he was associated with Phil May.

Back in England in the 1890s, he became associated with James Pryde and William Nicholson who revolutionised poster designs. Returning to Australia, Young was the first to introduce artistic poster designs in this country. He became fully recognised as a watercolour artist when he exhibited a series of impressions of Mount Buffalo.

Young exhibited at the Royal Academy and was elected a member of the Royal Institute of Painters in Water Colour and the Royal Society of British Artists before returning to Australia in 1923. In 1929, he was appointed art critic on the Melbourne *Herald*.

The display case containing the Ashes urn and associated items was given to the MCC in memory of Claude Ashton (Winchester, Cambridge, and Essex) and Roger Winlaw (Winchester, Cambridge, and Surrey) who together gave their lives for their country on 31 October 1942.

Cricket historians and millions of readers down the years have accepted *Wisden*'s advice on the Ashes which has been published annually and without change since 1954, apparently without question. Time then, at the centenary of their creation, to examine the *Wisden* story more closely:

The Ashes were originated in 1882 when, on 29 August, Australia defeated the full strength of England on English soil for the first time.

This is ambiguously phrased and would have been less confusing to have said: 'The story of the Ashes began . . .'

The Australians won by the narrow margin of seven runs and the following day, the Sporting Times *printed a mock obituary notice, written by Shirley Brooks, son of an editor of* Punch, *which read . . .*

This sentence is inaccurate in one instance and gives rise to more confusion in another. The *Sporting Times* was published the next Saturday and the mock obituary was written by Reginald Brooks.

The following winter, the Hon. Ivo Bligh, afterwards Lord Darnley, set out to Australia to recover these mythical Ashes . . .

Bligh sailed on 14 September—still in the English summer.

Australia won the first match by nine wickets, but England won the next two, and the real Ashes came into being when some Melbourne women burnt a bail used in the third game and presented the ashes in an urn to Bligh . . .

There seems no doubt that presentations were made to Bligh at various times during the tour, but who presented what, when, where, and how, are surely questions which beg debate.

When Lord Darnley died in 1927, the urn, by a bequest in his will, was given to MCC . . .

In Lord Darnley's will, however, there appears to be no reference to the Ashes, the urn, or MCC.

There it (the urn) stands permanently, together with the velvet bag in which the urn was originally given to Lord Darnley and the scorecard of the 1882 match.

There are indications that the velvet bag was given to Bligh *after* the Ashes. This is implied in Bligh's letter to Mrs Fletcher: '. . . The Ashes shall be consigned to it forthwith . . .'

Wisden Cricketers' Almanack was founded by John Wisden in 1864. The first issue was 112 pages and it has been published annually since then without interruption. A best-seller now, it takes up more than 5 cm of shelf space. Norman Preston, who died on 6 March 1980, edited the almanack for twenty-nine years from 1951. He succeeded his father, Hubert, who was the editor for eight years. Between them, father and son served *Wisden* for eighty-five years. Norman was once described by John Woodcock, of *The Times*, and now the eleventh editor of the almanack, as the Mr Pickwick of cricket.

John Wisden was assured of a place in cricket history before he produced the almanack. A fast bowler, despite his small stature, he took all ten wickets for the North against the South at Lord's in 1850. This rare feat was garnished by all his victims being clean bowled.

Ashes probably first became associated with cricket after the Commissioners of the Lord Protector of England, Oliver Cromwell, forbade the playing of 'Krickett' in Ireland by an order of 1656 and commanded all 'sticks and balls' to be burnt by the common hangman.

About ten years passed after the creation of the Ashes before the next published reference to them. Responsible for this was an Australian journalist and author, Clarence P. Moody. He wrote a book called *South Australian Cricket* and was also the first to collate the accepted list of Test matches. In listing these he made reference to the contests as being 'for the Ashes'.

This phrase was used in Australia for some years before it became colloquial in England. Indeed, it might never have caught on but for Sir Pelham Warner.

Pelham 'Plum' Francis Warner was ten years older than the Ashes—born in 1873 in Trinidad where his father had been Attorney-General. Plum became captain of cricket at Rugby School, gained a Blue at Oxford and played for Middlesex from 1894 until 1920.

He was elected to the committee of the Marylebone Cricket Club in 1904 and remained on it for most of the rest of his life. His name became synonymous with the MCC and Lord's. In 1903, he announced his intention to 'recover the Ashes'—again, and captained the first official MCC team to Australia in 1903–04. On his victorious return, against expectations, he wrote a book, *How We Recovered The Ashes*, which has been emulated many times since. But it was Plum's initiative which led to the phrase taking root in the English popular vocabulary. In 1937, Warner was knighted for his services to the game. He was well read, scholarly, and founded *The Cricketer* which he edited for some years. He died in 1963 and is commemorated by the Warner Stand at Lord's.

Although the MCC's story of The Ashes and their catalogue both refer to a pottery urn, Sir Pelham, in his history of Lord's in 1946, thought differently:

'. . . but the fact remains that he (Ivo Bligh) was presented, in Australia, with a gold urn with the ashes of burnt cricket stumps; and the urn, with the ashes inside, is to be seen in a glass case in the Long Room in Lord's . . .'

By 1951, however, Sir Pelham, in the *Sportsman's Handbook*, had decided that the urn was pottery. But the White Lion Publishers, when they brought out a new edition of Sir Pelham's history in 1974, stuck to his original conclusion that the urn was gold after all.

That the original urn might have been of gold is not an impossibility. Certainly Sir William Clarke could easily have afforded it and was capable of such extravagance. It should be remembered also that at the Christmas Day ball at Rupertswood in 1882, Lady Janet Clarke presented iron, gold, and steel souvenirs of the *Peshawur* to the Englishmen. As far as is known, there is no record of exactly what those souvenirs were, but a gold urn could have been one of them. If the original urn was gold, then what happened to it?

The household status of the term 'The Ashes' was further strengthened after Florence, the Dowager Countess of Darnley, gave the urn to the MCC in 1929. It is believed that previously it had been kept in the Darnley family homes, first at Cobham Hall and then in Puckle Hill House, Shorne.

In the Long Room in the pavilion at Lord's, the urn came under the eye of a much bigger but still exclusive audience, that is the members of the MCC and their guests. The urn rested here until 1953 when it was moved the few metres to the cricket museum behind the pavilion.

The Brooks and the Blighs probably never met, but they had a mutual acquaintance in Charles Dickens. Shirley Brooks wrote in his diary on Tuesday, 5 January 1865: 'Emily heard Dickens read "Nancy" — she was not impressed.' Another entry noted Emily having received an invitation from Mrs Dickens to be godparent to the novelist's last child. According to Shirley, he could see no way to refuse without causing offence. Emily went along reluctantly to the christening.

Lord Darnley gave Dickens keys to the gates of Cobham Park and the novelist once took William Longfellow's eldest daughter, Alice, for a drive there. She was thrilled by the undulating turf, the great trees up to their knees in ferns, and the little rabbits dashing around. The park was one of Dickens' favourite places in which to relax, and his last walk was taken through it before he died.

When a lecture tour to Australia by Dickens was cancelled in the early 1860s, it was replaced by the first touring side of English cricketers. They were sponsored by Spiers and Ponds, the catering firm for Melbourne Cricket Club. But the first Test was not held until 1877. It began in Melbourne on 15 March and the first delivery was bowled by Alfred Shaw to Charles Bannerman, the elder brother of Alec. Australia won the first of the three-match series by 45 runs. England won the second by four wickets and Australia won the decider by ten wickets. All three were played in Melbourne.

Then came the first Test in England — at The Oval — in 1880, England winning by five wickets to square the account. The next Test was in

Melbourne again and this ended as a draw on 4 January 1882. Sydney staged its first Test from 17–21 February that year and its second from 3–7 March. Australia won both of them. The next Test, back in Melbourne from 10–14 March, was drawn and so Australia won that series 2–0. Thus Test cricket arrived at the threshold of the Ashes saga with Australia still needing to beat England in England.

CHAPTER 14

Like a weary but still-proud grandmother, Cobham Hall today seems quietly to draw sustenance from reflection on its Victorian heyday. Still guarded by brooding woods, but owned now by the Westwood Educational Trust, it nestles in Kentish parkland only 43 kilometres from the hive of London and a healthy jog from a reach of the Thames where the old river, sensing journey's end, begins to feel for the pulse of the sea.

A path hacked by the author through a forgotten jungle corner of Cobham churchyard to the grave of Ivo and Florence

A kilometre or two from the Hall, Ivo and Florence rest in peace in the neglected south-east corner of Cobham churchyard. They are only a few steps from the Leather Bottle Inn, crammed with Dickensiana, on narrow Main Street. Their gravestone is hidden by a tangle of roses, ivy, elderberry, and nettles. That they should be in this place was not the intention of the third Earl of Darnley who built, deep in Cobham Woods, a private family mausoleum. The building was about to be consecrated by the Bishop of Rochester when a thunderstorm broke. After the storm, His Grace regarded this as a bad omen and refused to conduct the consecration ceremony. Consequently, the Darnleys continued to be buried in the village churchyard. In the church is a magnificent stained-glass window in memory of the

Cobham Church, Kent, England

143

Darnleys. Today, the mausoleum is an empty shell defaced by graffiti. Sometimes it echoes to the roar of motor-cycles bucking along the woodland tracks. A sapling struggles for life from a cleft in the domed roof and the only regular visitors to this eerie ruin are perhaps owls and other wild creatures of the woods.

On the other side of the world, Beechworth, in northern Victoria, boasts of being the State's best-preserved gold town. It is more concerned with the legend of the bushranger, Ned Kelly, than the eighth Countess of Darnley.

Kelly, of course, met his Waterloo at neighbouring Glenrowan on the Hume Highway, but before this, Beechworth was one of his regular haunts and one of his associates came from the town.

Kelly languished for some time in gaol at Beechworth and this building in the town is among more than thirty classified or recorded by the National Trust. Each has its story to proclaim.

Less obvious are the surviving traces of John Stephen Morphy and his family. His grave, masked by rubbish, is surrounded by rusting railings near the gazebo in the town's cemetery.

In the shire council offices, there survive records of the rates paid by the Morphys for their property in Havelock Road and a tiny photograph of John Morphy can be found among a collage of the town's historic personalities on display in the Burke Museum in Loch Street.

Havelock Road is still a dirt track. It gives access from both sides to several small farms which are plagued from time to time by a small mob of kangaroos. One of these properties is owned by Mr and Mrs W. Denisenko. There are traces of several other long-demolished buildings on this site. One of these, or even a part of the house standing there today, was the building in which Florence Morphy spent at least part of her childhood.

The currently best-preserved item of Morphy memorabilia in Beechworth is the *Book of Common Prayer* cared for by Father Malcolm Crawley at Christ Church Rectory, in Ford Street. The book is inscribed: 'Presented to Christ Church, Beechworth, by the Countess of Darnley in memory of her father, John Stephen Morphy. February 1904.'

Florence visited Australia at that time, accompanied by her third and last child, Lady Dorothy. They had sailed from England in the P & O liner *Ophir*. There is also the record of Florence's christening in the parish register of births.

South-west across the country from Beechworth is Rupertswood College, Sunbury. Above it, aircraft decide on the best approach to Tullamarine Airport, Melbourne.

As Sir William Clarke's country mansion, Rupertswood, was considered one of the grandest houses in Australia. For a few years, it played an official part in the defence of Australia and once added colour to a royal wedding in England.

There is little doubt that 'Big' Clarke would have disapproved of the extravagance that Rupertswood represented, but he had been dead for

Rupertswood College, Sunbury, Victoria

several months when his daughter-in-law, Mary Clarke, William's first wife, laid the foundation stone on 29 August 1874.

The mansion, with a tower rising more than 30 metres, was completed in 1876. It had fifty rooms and the most eye-catching feature of the foyer was Japanese stained glass depicting Australian hunting scenes. Over a magnificent ballroom was a dormitory in which visiting cricketers slept. The house stood in a paradise of gardens behind an ornamental lake fashioned in the shape of Australia. A rail track branched to the estate, thus enabling trains to bring guests from Melbourne. First to arrive in this manner were 400 workmen who had been involved in the building.

The former ballroom, now a chapel, at Rupertswood, Sunbury, Victoria

In the late 1880s, Sir William, as he was by then, saw, along with others, a threat to Australia from Russia. Consequently, he founded, with the approval of the State Government, Nordenfelt Battery of Victorian Horse Artillery—named after the three Nordenfelt field pieces with which he equipped the battery. These Swedish-designed weapons were among the earliest type of successful machine-gun.

Sir William maintained the unit—soon popularly known as the Rupertswood Battery—from his own pocket at an annual cost of what today would be more than $300 000.

In 1893, Sir William sent his 'army' to Britain where it took part successfully in various military tournaments and was presented to Queen Victoria. The unit's final official duty in England was to act as military escort for the marriage of the Duke of York and Princess Mary of Teck, the future King George V and Queen Mary. The battery was eventually disbanded in 1897 after the State Government had refused to help Sir Rupert Clarke support it.

Rupertswood itself was sold by the Hon. Russell Clarke in 1922. In 1927, the estate was bought by its present owners, the Salesians—a Roman Catholic teaching order which maintains a pride in the estate's historic significance and offers a range of educational opportunities to some 500 students.

In 1977, the battery was reformed at the college as a cadet corps and so, almost 100 years after first parading, 'soldiers' in rippling blue and gold can still be seen to patrol and defend Rupertswood.

Today, ducks and other waterbirds bob and gossip beside the lake and horses graze in an area between the house and the railway track which was once known as the cricket paddock.

In the early 1980s, the Clarkes of Melbourne are pacesetters in Victorian society—especially the dynamic Lady Kathleen Clarke, wife of Sir Rupert, the present head of the family. The second Sir Rupert, a great-grandson of 'Big' Clarke, and a cousin of Mr Michael Clarke, is a retiring but multi-millionaire businessman.

Sir Rupert's possessions include the 2000-hectare property, Bolinda Vale, at Clarkefield, but their home in Melbourne, the Georgian Richmond House in South Yarra, is owned by Lady Clarke. She bought it about 1958 with money inherited from her brewery family.

Today, Lady Clarke is a charity organiser, art collector, racehorse owner, cattle breeder, maker of cumquat marmalade, and darner of socks. The Clarkes often entertain VIPs for the Government. Once, when a prince was to visit for the weekend, Lady Clarke decided that there ought to be koalas in the Bolinda Vale gum trees around her garden. She made a telephone call and the Wildlife Service provided them.

In 1980 the *Age* newspaper reported: '. . . Apart from elephant tusks over the fireplace, Bolinda Vale also houses one of Ned Kelly's four suits of armour, a patch where Burke and Wills slept on their trek north, and a patch where the bails were burnt to make the legendary Ashes . . .'

Bolinda Vale is managed by the Clarkes' eldest son and heir to the family title, Rupert Clarke. However, Mr Clarke, and his wife, Sussanah, profess ignorance of any 'patch' where the Ashes were burned.

Lady Clarke also denies the existence of any such patch at Bolinda Vale. She volunteers, however, the belief that Lady Janet Clarke had organised the burning of the Ashes, presented them to Ivo Bligh and intended that they should be held by England or Australia, according to the swing of fortunes on the cricket field. At the same time, Lady Clarke shies from the possibility that the Ashes were burned at Rupertswood, only a few kilometres from Bolinda Vale.

In sharp contrast to the Clarkes, the present Earl of Darnley, Adam Ivo Stuart Bligh, lives very quietly at Puckle Hill House, Shorne, overlooking the former family seat near Gravesend in Kent.

How important are the Ashes? Although the old debate among cricket historians as to whether Ivo Bligh recovered the Ashes or not seems to have faded, the Ashes can still fire controversy and make headlines without a ball being bowled.

The authorities at Lord's apparently agonised for days in October 1979 before making a decision about the Ashes for the three-Test series in Australia in 1979–80. At that time, a member of the Australian Cricket Board of Control, Mr Ray Steele, said that England's indecision on whether or not to play for the Ashes was ridiculous.

The secretary of the Test and County Cricket Board, Mr Donald Carr, replied: 'I am disappointed and surprised by some of Mr Steele's comments and I hope they will not be allowed to affect the good relationship between the two countries.'

In the *Guardian* newspaper, John Arlott said that the authorities would be 'straining at a gnat' not to put the Ashes at stake.

In the *Yorkshire Post*, Terry Brindle said: '. . . having agreed to wear Packer-style coloured pads and gloves for the benefit of the TV cameras, England may well feel that they are entitled to preserve some traditional atmosphere by refusing to stake the Ashes over a three-match series.'

Brindle said he understood that England had agreed unofficially to play for the Ashes, but the decision had to be ratified by the TCCB chairman's advisory committee.

In the *Guardian*, Arlott also said that the coming series was 'a far more valid contest between the two countries, than that in Australia last season when England, without Woolmer, Underwood, Knott, and Amiss, beat Australia without any of their twenty-odd Packer players.'

In the event, the TCCB refused to put the Ashes at stake, but many Australians regarded them at stake anyway. Australia went on to win 3–0 the series against an England team led by Michael Brearley.

In the Test series for the Ashes in England in 1981, the home side won 3–1 with two matches drawn. While some authorities claimed that England had *regained* the Ashes, others maintained that they had been *retained.*

So as long as Australia and England confront each other on a cricket field there is likely to be a spark among the Ashes, ensuring that Reginald and Ivo and Florence are never completely forgotten. A few may also spare a thought for Shirley and Emily, and for Cecil Brooks, wherever he rests. Sir William Clarke, of course, is remembered by all who gaze on his statue outside the Treasury in Melbourne, but not all of them will previously have associated him with the Ashes.

ADDITIONAL NOTE

On permanent display in the Melbourne Cricket Ground pavilion is a magnificent silver cricket trophy — The Sir Robert Menzies Memorial Trophy. It was commissioned by a former Australian High Commissioner in London, Sir John Bunting, and designed and made by Stuart Devlin who designed Australia's decimal coins.

The trophy is made of silver and silver gilt. It depicts a full team of eleven cricketers in various stances arranged around a tall spire. The stand is of rosewood with an engraved silver band.

Contrasting dramatically with the Ashes urn, it is competed for in a single match between England and the Australian Prime Minister's XI. But if England wins the trophy, the visitors cannot take it away. After the presentation, it must be handed back to the M.C.G. for safekeeping.

ACKNOWLEDGMENTS

The author wishes to thank for their help: The Hon. Michael Clarke, of Burnewang North, Rochester, Victoria; the former secretary of the Australian Cricket Board of Control, Mr Alan Barnes; Miss Joan M. Fletcher, Mrs Ruth Forth and other descendants in Brisbane, Queensland, of Mrs Ann Fletcher; Father Terence Francis Jennings and Father Julian Fox, of Rupertswood College, Sunbury, Victoria; Judith and Frank Worthy, of Mitcham, and Grant Aldous, of North Carlton, Victoria; Mr Geoff Craig, of Stanley, Victoria; Beechworthians (Victoria) generally and especially Mrs Leokardia Denisenko, of Havelock Road; Father Malcolm Crawley, Father Stockdale; the Burke Memorial Museum manager, Mr Reginald Brine; Mr and Mrs John Archer, Mrs Doreen Blake, the staff of the *Ovens and Murrey Advertiser*, the staff of the Beechworth Shire Hall (particularly Miss Elaine Howell and Mr Lee Holmes), Mrs Betty E. Hornsey; Ruth Schmedding, Senior Reference Librarian, National Library of Australia, Canberra; Bronwen Hughes, the La Trobe Library, Melbourne; the staff of the State Library and the Battye Library, Western Australia; the WA Newspaper Company Limited, and particularly Bruce Wroth, of Western Australia; Valerie and Michael Sales, of Morley, Western Australia; and his wife, Fiona Willis.

The Hon. Noel Bligh, of London; the secretary of the Marylebone Cricket Club, Mr J. A. Bailey; the Lord's Museum curator, Mr Stephen Green; the Surrey County Cricket Club secretary, Mr I. F. B. Scott-Brown; Mrs Lynne Friel, National Maritime Museum, London; Mrs P. Russell and Miss S. M. Bonvin, Lloyd's Register of Shipping, London; Mr Stephen Rabson, Group Librarian, P and O, London; Mr Maurice Smith, A.L.A., Principal Reference Librarian, York and Selby Division, North Yorkshire County Library, and his assistants; Peter Willis, the Gravesend Public Library; Nigel Talbot Rice, headmaster, Summer Fields, Oxford; Mr H. W. Clayton, Brighthampton, Witney, Oxon; Mr and Mrs John Morris, Kent Terrace, Baker Street, London; the library staff of *Punch* magazine, Tudor Street, London; and Cdre A. G. W. Bellars, Bursar, Westwood Educational Trust Limited, Cobham Hall, Cobham, Kent; and Mrs Faith Rimmer, of Gravesend, Kent; and Mr Patrick Eagar, of Kew, Richmond, England.

REFERENCES

Some sources not referred to in the text:

'Big' Clarke by Michael Clarke. Queensbury Hill Press, 1980.

The Lords of Cobham Hall by Esme Wingfield Stratford. Cassell, 1959.

Background to Beechworth by Roy C. Harvey. 1952.

The History of the Parish of Beechworth by Father Leo Lane. 1978.

The Complete Who's Who of Test Cricketers by Christopher Martin Jenkins. Rigby, 1980.

England Versus Australia: A Pictorial History by David Frith. ABC, 1980.

The Fast Men by David Frith. Horwitz Grahame, 1981.

Arlott and Trueman on Cricket. BBC, 1977.

SCOREBOARD

Australia won the toss, and the match by seven runs

AUSTRALIA

	FIRST INNINGS		SECOND INNINGS	
A. C. Bannerman	c Grace b Peate	9	c Studd b Barnes	13
H. H. Massie	b Ulyett	1	b Steel	55
W. L. Murdoch	b Peate	13	(4) run out	29
G. J. Bonnor	b Barlow	1	(3) b Ulyett	2
T. P. Horan	b Barlow	3	c Grace b Peate	2
G. Giffen	b Peate	2	c Grace b Peate	0
J. M. Blackham	c Grace b Barlow	17	c Lyttelton b Peate	7
T. W. Garrett	c Read b Peate	10	(10) not out	2
H. F. Boyle	b Barlow	2	(11) b Steel	0
S. P. Jones	c Barnes b Barlow	0	(8) run out	6
F. R. Spofforth	not out	4	(9) b Peate	0
Sundries	(b 1)	1	(b 6)	6
Total		63		122

Fall of wickets: 1/6; 2/21; 3/22; 4/26; 5/30; 6/30; 7/48; 8/51; 9/59; 10/63.
1/66; 2/70; 3/70; 4/79; 5/79; 6/99; 7/114; 8/117; 9/122; 10/122.

ENGLAND BOWLING:

	FIRST INNINGS				SECOND INNINGS			
	O	M	R	W	O	M	R	W
Peate	38	24	31	4	21	9	40	4
Ulyett	9	5	11	1	6	2	10	1
Barlow	31	22	19	5	13	5	27	0
Steel	2	1	1	0	7	0	15	2
Barnes					12	5	15	1
Studd					4	1	9	0

ENGLAND

	FIRST INNINGS		SECOND INNINGS	
R. G. Barlow	c Bannerman b Spofforth	11	(3) b Spofforth	0
W. G. Grace	b Spofforth	4	c Bannerman b Boyle	32
G. Ulyett	st Blackham b Spofforth	26	(4) c Blackham b Spofforth	11
A. P. Lucas	c Blackham b Boyle	9	(5) b Spofforth	5
A. Lyttelton	c Blackham b Spofforth	2	(6) b Spofforth	12
C. T. Studd	b Spofforth	0	(10) not out	0
J. M. Read	not out	19	(8) b Spofforth	0
W. Barnes	b Boyle	5	(9) c Murdoch b Boyle	2
A. G. Steel	b Garrett	14	(7) c and b Spofforth	0
A. N. Hornby	b Spofforth	2	(1) b Spofforth	9
E. Peate	c Boyle b Spofforth	0	b Boyle	2
Sundries	(b6, lb 2, nb 1)	9	(b 3, nb 1)	4
Total		101		77

153

Fall of wickets: 1/13; 2/18; 3/57; 4/59; 5/60; 6/63; 7/70; 8/96; 9/101; 10/101.
1/15; 2/15; 3/51; 4/53; 5/66; 6/70; 7/70; 8/75; 9/75; 10/77.

AUSTRALIA BOWLING:

	FIRST INNINGS				SECOND INNINGS			
	O	M	R	W	O	M	R	W
Spofforth	36·3	18	46	7	28	15	44	7
Garrett	16	7	22	1	7	2	10	0
Boyle	19	7	24	2	20	11	19	3

Umpires: R. Thoms and L. Greenwood.

FIRST TEST, 1882–83, (MELBOURNE) 30 DECEMBER AND 1 AND 2 JANUARY
Australia won the toss, and the match by nine wickets

AUSTRALIA

	FIRST INNINGS		SECOND INNINGS	
A. C. Bannerman	st Tylecote b Leslie	30	not out	25
H. H. Massie	c and b C. T. Studd	4	c and b Barnes	0
W. L. Murdoch	b Leslie	48	not out	33
T. P. Horan	c Barlow b Leslie	0		
P. S. McDonnell	b Bates	43		
G. Giffen	st Tylecote b Steel	36		
G. J. Bonnor	c Barlow b Barnes	85		
J. M. Blackham	c Tylecote b C. T. Studd	25		
F. R. Spofforth	c Steel b Barnes	9		
T. W. Garrett	c C. T. Studd b Steel	0		
G. E. Palmer	not out	0		
Sundries	(b 4, lb 2, w 2, nb 3)	11		
Total		291	(1 wkt) 58	

Fall of wickets: 1/5; 2/81; 3/81; 4/96; 5/162; 6/190; 7/251; 8/289; 9/289; 10/291.
1/0.

ENGLAND BOWLING:

	FIRST INNINGS				SECOND INNINGS			
	O	M	R	W	O	M	R	W
C. T. Studd	46	30	35	2	14	11	7	0
Barnes	30	11	51	2	13	8	6	1
Steel	33	16	68	2	9	4	17	0
Barlow	20	6	37	0	4	2	6	0
Bates	21	7	31	1	13·1	7	22	0
Read	8	2	27	0				
Leslie	11	1	31	3				

ENGLAND

	FIRST INNINGS		SECOND INNINGS	
R. G. Barlow	st Blackham b Palmer	10	b Spofforth	28
I. F. W. Bligh	b Palmer	0	(5) b Spofforth	3
C. F. H. Leslie	c Garrett b Palmer	4	(7) b Giffen	4
C. T. Studd	b Spofforth	0	(3) b Palmer	21
A. G. Steel	b Palmer	27	(4) lbw b Giffen	29
W. W. Read	b Palmer	19	b Giffen	29
W. Bates	c Bannerman b Garrett	28	(8) c Massie b Palmer	11
E. F. S. Tylecote	b Palmer	33	(2) b Spofforth	38
G. B. Studd	run out	7	c Palmer b Giffen	0
W. Barnes	b Palmer	26	not out	2
G. F. Vernon	not out	11	lbw b Palmer	3
Sundries	(b 8, lb 1, nb 3)	12	(lb 1)	1
Total		177		169

Fall of wickets: 1/2; 2/7; 3/8; 4/36; 5/45; 6/96; 7/96; 8/117; 9/156; 10/177.
1/64; 2/75; 3/105; 4/108; 5/132; 6/150; 7/164; 8/164; 9/164; 10/169.

AUSTRALIA BOWLING:

	FIRST INNINGS				SECOND INNINGS			
	O	M	R	W	O	M	R	W
Spofforth	28	11	56	1	41	15	65	3
Palmer	52·2	25	65	7	36·1	11	61	3
Garrett	27	6	44	1	2	1	4	0
Giffen					20	7	38	4

Umpires: J. Swift and E. H. Elliott.

SECOND TEST, 1883 (MELBOURNE) 19, 20 AND 22 JANUARY
England won the toss, and the match by an innings and 27 runs

ENGLAND

	FIRST INNINGS		SECOND INNINGS
R. G. Barlow	b Palmer	14	
C. T. Studd	b Palmer	14	
C. F. H. Leslie	run out	54	
A. G. Steel	c McDonnell b Giffen	39	
W. W. Read	c and b Palmer	75	
W. Barnes	b Giffen	32	
E. F. S. Tylecote	b Giffen	0	
I. F. W. Bligh	b Giffen	0	
W. Bates	c Horan b Palmer	55	
G. B. Studd	b Palmer	1	
F. Morley	not out	0	
Sundries	(b 3, lb 3, nb 4)	10	
Total		294	

Fall of wickets: 1/28; 2/35; 3/106; 4/131; 5/193; 6/199; 7/199; 8/287; 9/293; 10/294.

AUSTRALIA BOWLING:

FIRST INNINGS

	O	M	R	W
Spofforth	34	11	57	0
Palmer	66·3	25	103	5
Giffen	49	13	89	4
Garrett	34	16	35	0

AUSTRALIA

	FIRST INNINGS		SECOND INNINGS	
H. H. Massie	b Barlow	43	(7) c C. T. Studd b Barlow	10
A. C. Bannerman	b Bates	14	c Bligh b Bates	14
W. L. Murdoch	not out	19	(1) b Bates	17
T. P. Horan	c and b Barnes	3	(5) c Morley b Bates	15
P. S. McDonnell	b Bates	3	(6) b Bates	13
G. Giffen	c and b Bates	0	(8) c Bligh b Bates	19
G. J. Bonnor	c Read b Bates	0	(4) c Morley b Barlow	34
J. M. Blackham	b Barnes	5	(3) b Barlow	6
T. W. Garrett	b Bates	10	c Barnes b Bates	6
G. E. Palmer	b Bates	7	c G. B. Studd b Bates	4
F. R. Spofforth	b Bates	0	not out	14
Sundries	(b 6, lb 3, nb 1)	10	(b 1)	1
Total		114		153

Fall of wickets: 1/56; 2/72; 3/75; 4/78; 5/78; 6/78; 7/85; 8/104; 9/114; 10/114.
      1/21; 2/28; 3/66; 4/72; 5/93; 6/104; 7/113; 8/132; 9/139; 10/153.

ENGLAND BOWLING:

	FIRST INNINGS				SECOND INNINGS			
	O	M	R	W	O	M	R	W
C. T. Studd	4	1	22	0				
Morley	23	16	13	0	2	0	7	0
Barnes	23	7	32	2	3	1	4	0
Barlow	22	18	9	1	31	6	67	3
Bates	26·2	14	28	7	33	14	74	7

Umpires: J. Swift and E. H. Elliott.

THIRD TEST, 1883 (SYDNEY) 26, 27, 29 AND 30 JANUARY
England won the toss, and the match by 69 runs

ENGLAND

	FIRST INNINGS		SECOND INNINGS	
R. G. Barlow	c Murdoch b Spofforth	28	(3) c Palmer b Horan	24
C. T. Studd	c Blackham b Garrett	21	b Spofforth	25
C. F. H. Leslie	b Spofforth	0	(1) b Spofforth	8
A. G. Steel	b Garrett	17	lbw b Spofforth	6
W. W. Read	c Massie b Bannerman	66	b Horan	21
W. Barnes	b Spofforth	2	lbw b Spofforth	3
E. F. S. Tylecote	run out	66	c Bonnor b Spofforth	0
W. Bates	c McDonnell b Spofforth	17	c Murdoch b Horan	4
G. B. Studd	b Palmer	3	(10) c Garrett b Spofforth	8
I. F. W. Bligh	b Palmer	13	(9) not out	17
F. Morley	not out	2	b Spofforth	0
Sundries	(b 8, lb 3, nb 1)	12	(b 5, lb 2)	7
Total		247		123

Fall of wickets: 1/41; 2/44; 3/67; 4/69; 5/75; 6/191; 7/223; 8/224; 9/244; 10/247.
1/13; 2/45; 3/55; 4/87; 5/94; 6/94; 7/97; 8/98; 9/115; 10/123.

AUSTRALIA BOWLING:

	FIRST INNINGS				SECOND INNINGS			
	O	M	R	W	O	M	R	W
Giffen	12	3	37	0				
Palmer	38	21	38	2	9	3	19	0
Spofforth	51	19	73	4	41·1	23	44	7
Garrett	27	8	54	2	13	3	31	0
Bannerman	11	2	17	1				
McDonnell	4	0	16	0				
Horan					17	10	22	3

AUSTRALIA

	FIRST INNINGS		SECOND INNINGS	
A. C. Bannerman	c Bates b Morley	94	c Bligh b Barlow	5
G. Giffen	st Tylecote b Bates	41	b Barlow	7
W. L. Murdoch	lbw b Steel	19	c G. B. Studd b Morley	0
P. S. McDonnell	b Steel	0	(5) c Bligh b Morley	0
T. P. Horan	c Steel b Morley	19	(4) run out	8
H. H. Massie	c Bligh b Steel	1	c C. T. Studd b Barlow	11
G. J. Bonnor	c G. B. Studd b Morley	0	b Barlow	8
J. M. Blackham	b Barlow	27	b Barlow	26
T. W. Garrett	c Barlow b Morley	0	(11) b Barlow	0
G. E. Palmer	c G. B. Studd b Barnes	7	not out	2
F. R. Spofforth	not out	0	(9) c Steel b Barlow	7
Sundries	(b 6, lb 2, nb 1, w 1)	10	(b 6, lb 2, w 1)	9
Total		218		83

Fall of wickets: 1/76; 2/140; 3/140; 4/176; 5/177; 6/178; 7/196; 8/196; 9/218; 10/218.
1/11; 2/12; 3/18; 4/18; 5/30; 6/33; 7/56; 8/72; 9/80; 10/83.

ENGLAND BOWLING:

	FIRST INNINGS				SECOND INNINGS			
	O	M	R	W	O	M	R	W
Morley	34	16	47	4	35	19	34	2
Barlow	47·1	31	52	1	34·2	20	40	7
Bates	45	20	55	1				
Barnes	13	6	22	1				
C. T. Studd	14	11	5	0				
Steel	26	14	27	3				

Umpires: J. Swift and E. H. Elliott.

FOURTH TEST, 1883 (SYDNEY) 17, 19, 20, 21 FEBRUARY
England won the toss. Australia won the match by four wickets

ENGLAND

	FIRST INNINGS		SECOND INNINGS	
R. G. Barlow	c Murdoch b Midwinter	2	c Bonnor b Midwinter	20
C. T. Studd	run out	48	c Murdoch b Midwinter	31
C. F. H. Leslie	c Bonnor b Boyle	17	b Horan	19
A. G. Steel	not out	135	b Spofforth	21
W. W. Read	c Bonnor b Boyle	11	b Spofforth	7
E. F. S. Tylecote	b Boyle	5	b Palmer	0
W. Barnes	b Spofforth	2	(9) c and b Boyle	20
W. Bates	c Bonnor b Midwinter	9	(7) not out	48
I. F. W. Bligh	b Palmer	19	(8) c Murdoch b Horan	10
G. B. Studd	run out	3	c Murdoch b Boyle	9
F. Morley	b Palmer	0	c Blackham b Palmer	2
Sundries	(b 4, lb 7, nb 1)	12	(b 8, lb 1, nb 1)	10
Total		263		197

Fall of wickets: 1/13; 2/37; 3/110; 4/150; 5/156; 6/159; 7/199; 8/236; 9/263; 10/263.
1/54; 2/55; 3/77; 4/99; 5/100; 6/112; 7/137; 8/178; 9/192; 10/197.

AUSTRALIA BOWLING:

	FIRST INNINGS				SECOND INNINGS			
	O	M	R	W	O	M	R	W
Palmer	24	9	52	2	43·3	19	59	2
Midwinter	47	24	50	2	23	13	21	2
Spofforth	21	8	56	1	28	6	57	2
Boyle	40	19	52	3	23	6	35	2
Horan	12	4	26	0	9	2	15	2
Evans	11	3	15	0				

AUSTRALIA

	FIRST INNINGS			SECOND INNINGS	
A. C. Bannerman	c Barlow b Morley	10		c Bligh b C. T. Studd	63
G. J. Bonnor	c Barlow b Steel	87		(3) c G. B. Studd b Steel	3
W. L. Murdoch	b Barlow	0		(2) c Barlow b Bates	17
T. P. Horan	c G. B. Studd b Morley	4		c and b Bates	0
G. Giffen	c G. B. Studd b Leslie	27		st Tylecote b Steel	32
W. E. Midwinter	b Barlow	10		(8) not out	8
J. M. Blackham	b Bates	57		(6) not out	58
G. E. Palmer	c Bligh b Steel	0			
E. Evans	not out	22		(7) c Leslie b Steel	0
F. R. Spofforth	c Bates b Steel	1			
H. F. Boyle	c G. B. Studd b Barlow	29			
Sundries	(b 10, lb 3, w 2)	15		(b 10, lb 4, w 4)	18
Total		262		(6 wkts)	199

Fall of wickets: 1/31; 2/34; 3/39; 4/113; 5/128; 6/160; 7/164; 8/220; 9/221; 10/262.
 1/44; 2/51; 3/51; 4/107; 5/162; 6/164.

ENGLAND BOWLING:

	FIRST INNINGS				SECOND INNINGS			
	O	M	R	W	O	M	R	W
Barlow	48	21	88	3	37·1	20	44	0
Morley	44	25	45	2	12	9	4	0
Barnes	10	2	33	0	16	5	22	0
Bates	15	6	24	1	39	19	52	2
Leslie	5	2	11	1	8	7	2	0
Steel	19	6	34	3	43	9	49	3
C. T. Studd	6	2	12	0	8	4	8	1

Umpires: J. Swift and E. H. Elliott.